T0318706

Cambridge Elements ≡

Elements in Corporate Governance
edited by
Thomas Clarke
UTS Business School, University of Technology Sydney

CORPORATE GOVERNANCE AND LEADERSHIP

The Board as the Nexus of Leadership-in-Governance

Monique Cikaliuk
University of Auckland

Ljiljana Eraković
University of Auckland

Brad Jackson
University of Waikato

Chris Noonan
University of Auckland

Susan Watson
University of Auckland

CAMBRIDGE
UNIVERSITY PRESS

CAMBRIDGE
UNIVERSITY PRESS

University Printing House, Cambridge CB2 8BS, United Kingdom

One Liberty Plaza, 20th Floor, New York, NY 10006, USA

477 Williamstown Road, Port Melbourne, VIC 3207, Australia

314–321, 3rd Floor, Plot 3, Splendor Forum, Jasola District Centre,
New Delhi – 110025, India

79 Anson Road, #06–04/06, Singapore 079906

Cambridge University Press is part of the University of Cambridge.

It furthers the University's mission by disseminating knowledge in the pursuit of
education, learning, and research at the highest international levels of excellence.

www.cambridge.org
Information on this title: www.cambridge.org/9781108815499
DOI: 10.1017/9781108895385

© Monique Cikaliuk, Ljiljana Eraković, Brad Jackson, Chris Noonan
and Susan Watson 2020

First published 2020

A catalogue record for this publication is available from the British Library.

ISBN 978-1-108-81549-9 Paperback
ISSN 2515-7175 (online)
ISSN 2515-7167 (print)

Cambridge University Press has no responsibility for the persistence or accuracy of
URLs for external or third-party internet websites referred to in this publication
and does not guarantee that any content on such websites is, or will remain,
accurate or appropriate.

Corporate Governance and Leadership

The Board as the Nexus of Leadership-in-Governance

Elements in Corporate Governance

DOI: 10.1017/9781108895385
First published online: July 2020

Monique Cikaliuk
University of Auckland

Ljiljana Eraković
University of Auckland

Brad Jackson
University of Waikato

Chris Noonan
University of Auckland

Susan Watson
University of Auckland

The authors are listed in alphabetical order.
Author for correspondence: Ljiljana Eraković, l.erakovic@auckland.ac.nz

Abstract: This Element deals with leadership and governance of corporations from the point of view of the board. We expand our understanding of board leadership by focusing on the modern company as a legal person comprised of a capital fund and the relationships among directors, shareholders, management and stakeholders. We propose a model which integrates insights from the fields of leadership and corporate governance and establishes a theoretical link illustrated by empirical findings in three intersections: team leadership on the board, the chair's leadership of the board and strategic leadership by the board. We maintain that this integrative model provides a powerful means to further an understanding of the board as the nexus of leadership and governance. We close this Element by identifying the new research directions that our integrative model opens up. We also identify the implications for practice for those who either serve on boards or provide support to them.

Keywords: board of directors; corporate governance; leadership; jurisprudence; corporate regulation

ISBNs: 9781108815499 (PB), 9781108895385 (OC)
ISSNs: 2515-7175 (online), 2515-7167 (print)

Contents

1 Introduction

Leadership and governance matter in creating organisations that work, especially during times of change. The dilemmas facing organisations are clearly revealed as markets become globally integrated, new forms of competition arise and digital technologies redefine the way that companies operate. In this context, companies can ill afford to stand still. Yet these developments create unprecedented challenges for the corporate practice of organisations and their boards. Routine, predictable approaches and conventional mindsets are unsuited for generating new ways of thinking and acting to deal with the transformations afoot.

For companies to survive and prosper, the importance of context is increasingly recognised as significant in understanding and practicing leadership and governance. Despite the long-standing focus in the areas of leadership and governance on similar phenomena, leadership and governance are rarely discussed together. Each area has evolved into a significant field of interest with developments taking place in parallel. As a result, the academic literature in each area has demonstrated a limited awareness of what is happening in the other area at the same time. What is beguiling about this isolation is that many boards of directors have shown that leadership in governance accords with and complements processes to develop companies that evolve with change.

There are undoubtedly many reasons for this persistent scholarly separation. One reason for such isolation is the disparate philosophical underpinnings which infuse leadership and corporate governance with resulting ways of thinking that shape domains of study and implicitly guide the kinds of questions for research and practice. Leadership is associated with the academic discipline of organisation studies and allied with organisational behaviour, psychology, psychoanalysis, sociology, economics, history and political science. Corporate governance is rooted in economics and law.

Another reason is the different world views or images of organisations that scholars working in different disciplines adopt (Morgan, 1997). The 'cultural view' shows how the image of organisation rests in shared meanings, which is closely allied with leadership and its emphasis on people and their interrelationships. A very different view is typically taken in corporate governance. The 'machine metaphor' focuses on an organisation as the relationship between structures, roles and technology which highlights policies and procedures over other dimensions. The images or world views show how a range of complementary and competing insights about the nature of organisations can be generated and how they can be governed and led.

It is difficult to put a finger on a single reason for the disciplinary-specific scholarly tradition. An outcome, however, of the separation is that researchers perpetuate ingrained assumptions to shape theoretical and empirical orientations for inquiry. As a result, perspectives and assumptions create, in partial ways, interesting insights that inform an understanding of leadership or governance. To phrase it another way, the foregrounding of ideas and insights by one perspective or theory creates a background. Other insights, ideas and perspectives are consigned to the background, far from clear view. This process has largely precluded scholars from considering how new questions and different theoretical perspectives could mutually complement and build on the work of others to broaden and deepen an understanding of leadership in governance.

The origin of this Element lies within a broader project to reinvigorate the study and practice of corporate governance and leadership by boards. This project is based on the belief that the corporate board plays an underappreciated leadership role in corporations. That the board acts as leader is a notion universally accepted in business and management schools but denied by agency theory and the private law understandings of the corporation.

The inner workings of the board have tended to be a black box to researchers. An impetus for this research arises, in part, from a desire to illustrate board leadership enacted in governance. Listed companies and those seeking to be listed through a partial change in ownership lend themselves to a concise set of empirical and conceptual inquiries for this Element than might otherwise occur. Based on our research, we outline a framework of leadership in governance, illustrating and discussing different aspects of leadership by the board. This Element acknowledges the distinct roots of each field in the disciplines of law and organisational studies that inform the origins of the project and establishes the salient differences that distinguish them. It makes the case that an integration of constructs between leadership and governance offers important opportunities for dialogue, empirical research and theoretical development for scholars interested in understanding the board as a nexus for leadership. The Element does not aim to provide a new theory of board leadership; rather, it is integrative, making the case that there is much to be learned from each discipline. This approach encourages researchers to expand the literature bases from which they draw to further cross-fertilise and advance an understanding of the board as the nexus of leadership and governance.

Identifying some of the influences that perpetuate the scholarly isolation of leadership and corporate governance research in this first section helps to explain the interdisciplinary approach taken in this Element. The remaining sections of this Element are organised as follows: Section 2 places the interdisciplinary approach in broad perspective and sets the theoretical and analytical foundation for the board as the nexus in which leadership and governance intersect. Section 3 provides an orientation to key theoretical debates through a legal lens that focuses on the nature of the modern corporation as a legal person comprised of a capital fund, arguing that the board must be taken into account for how the company might be governed in a principled way. Section 4 analyses what economic theory does and does not tell us about leadership in the corporation and links the leadership role of the board to its theoretical and empirical underpinnings. Section 5 introduces our integrative model and explains the linkages between organisational studies and legal disciplinary insights that inform our understandings of board leadership in governance. Section 6 provides empirical evidence, illustrating three intersections in which boards enact leadership in governance: team leadership on the board, the chair's leadership of the board and strategic leadership by the board. Section 7 examines recent developments in board leadership research and highlights the role of board leadership in strategy making. The final section, Section 8, draws together the themes of this Element to suggest avenues for future research and implications for practice for those who serve on boards or provide support to them.

2 Our Work of Integrating Knowledge in Researching Boards

The board of directors, as a research topic, has its foundations in the field of corporate governance, dominated by the disciplines of law and economics, and the discipline of organisation studies,[1] which includes the fields of organisational behaviour, strategy and leadership, among others.

Each of these academic perspectives offers a distinct position on the role, tasks and functions of a governing body. Typically, the corporate governance field has focused on a board's formal and structural characteristics, and its governance actors (directors, managers and shareholders) (Adams, Hermalin & Weisbach, 2010). The research in this tradition has mainly investigated governance mechanisms in relation to formal incentives (such as contracts) and monitoring structures (Westphal & Zajac, 2013) which can produce positive organisational performance. According to this view, the company is regarded as a nexus of contracts, and the board of directors is treated as a control mechanism whose main role is to monitor corporate management. Yet theory and practice of

---

[1] In social science research, organisation studies is considered a discipline (see Clegg & Bailey, 2007; Zahra & Newey, 2009). It has its intellectual roots in economics, sociology, psychology, anthropology and political science and includes fields such as management, organisational theory, organisational behaviour, strategy and leadership, among others.

corporate governance has undergone significant reforms, recognising the limitations of their own evangelisation.

From the corporate law point of view, there have been major discussions about where the fiduciary obligations of directors rest – with the shareholders or the corporation. Traditionally (and in the economic literature (see Adams, Hermalin & Weisbach, 2010, p. 91)), directors have a duty to protect the interests of the shareholders, but, as Weinstein (2013) has noted, in most of the countries in the Anglo-American legal domain, 'directors must act in the interests of corporation' (p. 52). Hence, this distinction marks two important advancements in the legal understanding of boards. First, it is directors' not managers' responsibility to decide what are the real interests of the corporation. In her widely cited book *The Shareholder Value Myth*, Lynn Stout (2012) clearly emphasised that 'The objective of any particular corporation may be best determined not by regulators, judges, or professors, or even by any individual shareholder or group of shareholders, but by a board of directors' (p. 115).

Second, in directing corporations, directors need to consider and appreciate the interests of various constituencies (stakeholders) who are directly involved in a corporation's economic activity, and whose interests are not always compatible. Thus, directors need not only balance the interests of shareholders and stakeholders but also different groups of non-shareholder stakeholders (see Clarke, 2013). These two arguments have major implications for views on duties and responsibilities of directors in a modern corporation, which we discuss in detail in Sections 3 and 5 of this Element.

Organisation studies scholars have changed their focus of attention from the board composition (Finkelstein & Mooney's (2003) 'four usual suspects') and its traditional consideration from the point of view of agency, stewardship, resource dependence or management hegemony theories, to behavioural aspects of board functioning. The research on boards in the last decade has become directed towards internal board dynamics, board relationships with various stakeholders and board value-adding activities (Huse, 2007, 2009, 2018). Accordingly, conceptual lenses have been broadened to include social network theory (e.g., McDonald, Khanna & Westphal, 2008; Nicholson, Alexander & Kiel, 2004), the team production model (e.g., Huse & Gabrielsson, 2012; Machold et al., 2011) and human and social capital theories (e.g., Khanna, Jones & Boivie, 2014; Kor & Sundaramurthy, 2009), among others, thus providing profound conceptual understandings of the work of boards of directors.

However, one of the critical lenses has surprisingly been neglected – leadership. We, the authors of this Element, are based in fields of corporate governance, leadership, organisation theory, corporate law and strategy. At the time when we started our conversations about boards of directors, in 2012, we noticed that there were no significant studies cross-fertilising research efforts between corporate governance and leadership (Erakovic & Jackson, 2012).

Given that a board sits at the apex of governance in any corporation directing (i.e., leading) an overall corporate strategy, this discovery surprised us. In learning about the preoccupations and approaches of each other's fields, we stressed the importance of 'crossing the boundaries' and integrating the work between the fields of corporate governance and leadership in order to gain a more comprehensive understanding of the work of boards of directors.

The strengths and weaknesses of these two fields, we argued (Erakovic & Jackson, 2012), complement each other when the work of the board is concerned. Corporate governance scholars have developed a sophisticated legal understanding of organisational relationships and have considerable experience working at its upper echelons. They have, however, tended to be constrained by an obsession with formal, static and impersonal conceptual models. Leadership, on the other hand, has traditionally been strong in casting light on significant informal, interpersonal dynamic processes within the middle and lower ranks of the organisation, but has tended to exclude boards from its conceptual and empirical focus. Therefore, crossing boundaries and creating a theoretical rapprochement between the two fields will have positive repercussions not only in terms of fresh empirical insights and comprehensive understanding but also in terms of improving and energising the everyday practice of corporate governance.

In terms of practice, corporate governance provides a formal structure for the relationships among organisational core constituencies, whereas leadership provides the energy and determination to make corporate governance effective in the achievement of the organisation's purpose and goals (Davies, 2006). Corporate governance sets the stage for leadership at the apex of the organisation and has an indirect but significant impact upon leadership processes at other levels within the organisation. In this respect, good leadership can revitalise corporate governance arrangements, while good governance can serve to sustain corporate leadership.

One feature that corporate governance and leadership have in common is their elusive nature when it comes to deciding on a common definition that can explain their scope and intent. It is arguable, though, that leadership holds a clear edge over governance in terms of its ambiguity and lack of agreement (Bryman et al., 2011). For the purpose of this Element, we define leadership as 'an influence relationship among leaders and followers who intend real changes that reflect their mutual purposes' (Rost, 1993, p. 10) and corporate governance as 'the process whereby people in power direct, monitor and lead corporations, and thereby either create, modify or destroy the structures and systems under which they operate' (McGregor, 2000, p. 11).[2]

In summary, this Element represents an attempt to encourage scholars from different fields and different parts of the world to look with new eyes at corporate governance concepts and take the next step in a research agenda that asks stimulating research questions, such as: 'What is the nature of a company in modern society?' and 'How is the board's work influenced in light of the previous question?' The 'nature of a company' is a conceptual area of law, whereas the 'work of the board' or 'board functioning' belongs more to organisation studies. The remaining sections of this Element analyse these conceptual issues that are fundamental to an improved understanding of the board as the nexus of corporate participants in greater detail and examine empirical evidence gained from those who are practicing governance in real organisations. The significance of our interdisciplinary approach is confirmed by a persistent call by businesses, professional associations and the academic community for a holistic (and more accurate) picture of governance practices.

3 What Is a Company? A View through a Legal Lens

What is a company and how should a company be governed, led and managed? These wicked questions sit at the centre of the study of the modern company. The answer to the first question should determine the answer to the secondary questions; it is only when we have a shared understanding of the essential nature of the company that we can hope to determine its governance in a principled way. In this section, we will set out our shared understanding of the structure of the modern company and, in doing so, explain why we have identified the board as the nexus of the company.

3.1 Theoretical Underpinnings

Two theories about the ultimate objective of the governance of the company currently compete: shareholder primacy theory, where it is argued that the company should be operated in the interests of shareholders, and stakeholder theory. Stakeholder theory advocates adopt an institutional position, arguing that the interests of all stakeholders should be balanced and accommodated

---

[2] We chose a definition which, for the purpose of our research and our arguments, stresses three important aspects of corporate governance: people (in power), leadership and outcomes (positive and negative). In our opinion, structures, mechanisms and processes emphasised in common corporate governance definitions are structural elements, not the core corporate governance function.

(Freeman, 1984; Gibson, 2000). The debate about the merits of the two theories is a long-standing one, perhaps epitomised by the exchange of articles on corporate accountability which took place between A. A. Berle and E. Merrick Dodd in the 1930s. It was Berle's view that corporate powers were powers in trust exercisable for the benefit of all the shareholders (Berle, 1931). Berle's early views may form the foundation of shareholder primacy theory (although Berle later resiled from a shareholder primacy conception of the company (Berle, 1965)). The classic Berle and Means corporation was based on a perception of the changed status of shareholders in large corporations where power had shifted to management. This change was characterised as a separation of ownership (by shareholders) from control (in management including directors). It provided the rationale for agency theory (Jensen & Meckling, 1976), which has dominated law-and-economics and to some extent corporate law policy since the 1980s. Dodd (1932), on the other hand, viewed corporations as economic institutions that had responsibilities not only to shareholders but also to employees, customers and the public. Dodd's arguments form the foundation of stakeholder theory (see the discussion in Attenborough, 2006).

These two competing theories about what normatively should be the objective of the company may be underpinned by different conceptions of the company. Many adherents of shareholder primacy conceive of the company as an association of shareholders who combine together and obtain corporate status through an incorporation statute. A logical consequence of this model is that management is perceived to be the agent of the shareholders, charged with acting in the best interests of the shareholders as a whole and as the company. The significance of the role of the board is ignored or downplayed as a monitor for equity investors, with little or no differentiation between directors and managers. Shareholders' interests are assumed to be shareholder wealth maximisation. The role of corporate law seen through this shareholder primacy lens is to minimise the agency problem, that was identified by Berle and Means, which is brought about by the separation of ownership from control (Jensen & Meckling, 1976).

We do not accept that shareholder wealth maximisation is the primary objective of the corporation or corporate law because we reject the conception of the company as being comprised of a contractually based association of shareholders. We also consider that the two key characteristics of the company, corporate legal personality and comprehensive limited liability, can only be derived from the state through the incorporation statute. The reasons for our stance are set out here. But we also do not base our work on a stakeholder conception of the company. In determining the objective of the governance of companies, stakeholder theorists generally do not consider that the interests of shareholders should be prioritised, arguing that shareholders are just another stakeholder in the company. Margaret Blair, for example, argued for a shift from contractual, exclusively profit-seeking entities ('property conception') of corporations to conceptualising them as social institutions that need to serve and balance interests of stakeholders beyond just shareholders (Blair, 1995, 1998). Blair asserted that such a shift would have important consequences for corporate governance, especially regarding management's accountability for, and monitoring of, the allocation of corporate resources.

In its broadest sense, 'a stakeholder in an organization is any group or individual who can affect or is affected by the achievement of the organization's objectives' (Freeman, 1984, p. 32). Stakeholder theorists conceive of the company as a type of organisation either surrounded by or comprised of a network of stakeholders. In general terms, scholars discuss normative and instrumental approaches to stakeholder theory (Donaldson & Preston, 1995; Kaler, 2003; Maharaj, 2008). The normative approach to stakeholder theory ('moral stakeholder theory') and corresponding governance orientation emphasise the board's true care for (duty to) all corporate stakeholders. Stakeholders have intrinsic value for the company. Therefore, the board makes true efforts to balance various stakeholders' interests and claims, and the board applies a participative and inclusive approach towards various stakeholder groups. The instrumental approach ('strategic stakeholder theory') stresses the corporate-centred approach (Maharaj, 2008), where the board puts the interest of the company first. These interests might be the interests of survival, profit maximisation, competitive advantage or risk minimisation. Hence, this governance orientation, although it may involve stakeholders' participation, leans towards stakeholder management rather than stakeholder engagement.

In fact, adherents to shareholder primacy also accept the importance of stakeholders while rejecting the argument that the company is an institution comprised of stakeholders. Markets are not frictionless and conflicts between different agents can reduce the value of the firm (Knoll, 2018). In other words, the value of the firm and the maximisation goal are influenced by actions of various internal and external stakeholders (who, with their diverse interests, make the market complex/non-frictionless). Therefore, even in a shareholder primacy model, shareholders will have to bear the agency costs directly associated with the specific governance arrangements employed to 'control' various stakeholder interests. The board's (and firm's) engagement with stakeholders incurs agency costs which, in the long run, influence the value of the firm. Even Michael Jensen, a major critic of stakeholder theory, suggests that 'A firm cannot maximise value if it ignores the interest of its stakeholders' (Jensen,

2001, p. 298). The interests of stakeholders are taken instrumentally as they need to be managed in order for a company to achieve its strategic objectives.

While seeing merit in both the normative and instrumental stakeholder approach to corporate governance, our stance is that stakeholder theory is based on an institutional model that does not recognise the distinct taxonomy of the modern company. Stakeholder theory does not set out what distinguishes the company from other forms of business organisation or institution. As discussed later, our model of the modern company is of an entity that is a capital fund that is given the status of a legal person.

3.1.1 Pitfalls of Shareholder Primacy

In rejecting a stakeholder conception of the company, we do not accept the alternative of shareholder primacy. Shareholder primacy theory is flawed in several fundamental ways. First, agency theory does not accurately describe company law. Corporate law has a complexity that the shareholder primacy theory does not identify and recognise. One of the precepts of agency theory and law is that the agent is accountable to the principal. Yet, in company law, directors as 'agents' are generally not accountable to shareholders as a 'principal' when acting as part of the board. Most jurisdictions have business judgement rules or principles where business decisions of directors are essentially not reviewable, so long as the directors comply with fiduciary obligations of loyalty and care, and avoid conflicts of interest. Moreover, the scope of the business judgement rule in the United States is so wide that the risk of liability for breach of the duty of care is virtually non-existent. Risk of liability for breach of the duty of care looms somewhat larger in the United Kingdom, Australia and New Zealand, but its application and enforcement are inconsistent. Either through the development and application of the business judgement rule, where courts will not retrospectively examine business decisions made by boards, or through the interpretation of a diverse array of statutory and common law rules from fiduciary duties to the unfair prejudice remedy for shareholders, courts have long avoided being forced to decide whether a particular company action maximises shareholder wealth.

It is clear, also, that shareholders as a class are, in fact, heterogeneous investors. Shareholders have different time horizons and invest for different purposes. Shareholders, directors and managers do not act with the pure and aligned aim of maximising shareholder wealth all of the time. Shareholders may, at times, be more focused on, for example, gaining control or growing the enterprise; directors may have a conflict of interest; management may wish to retain control and so forth. Many reasons explain such divergence, including opportunistic behaviour by directors and managers, strategic or personal interests of shareholders, bounded rationality of all participants and satisficing behaviour by all corporate participants, including the board.

Second, shareholder primacy theory fails to distinguish between directors and managers and, in doing so, fails to recognise the legal taxonomy of the company. Directors, when acting as part of the board as a primary organ or body of the company, have a different legal relationship to the company to when directors act as agents on behalf of the company. Directors are not always corporate agents. When directors act as part of the board of directors, their decisions are decisions of the company attributed to the company through the primary rules of attribution (*Meridian Global Funds Management Asia Ltd v. Securities Commission*, 1995 AC 2 (1995)).

Third, the existence of the classic Berle and Means corporation with separation of ownership and control may be the exception rather than the rule. The assumptions that most large firms are run by professional managers and that shareholders have relatively little say in the day-to-day operations or strategic decisions of the firm sit behind the property rights/contractual models of the firm (Burkart, Gromb & Panunzi, 1997). These assumptions do not hold in all or even most cases. The UK and US stock markets are now dominated by institutional investors, with the Australian stock market not too far behind. Individual investors have substantial shareholdings in most listed companies. Tech companies like Facebook and Amazon have founders who retain controlling stakes (see Davis, 2016). In many cases, boards do not act to maximise the wealth of the shareholders; instead, they pursue their own partisan interests or respond to immediate financial and other pressures. The coagulation of shareholdings in many corporations gives empirical weight to the research on boards and corporate governance that views firms as involving political bargaining among stakeholders (Deakin, 2019; Huse & Rindova, 2001). Shifting coalitions can affect corporate decisions and goals.

Fourth, the development of capital maintenance rules by the common law and statute in Commonwealth jurisdictions, as well as the more recent recognition that directors will owe duties to creditors when the company approaches insolvency, show that the equation of the interests of the company with the financial interests of the shareholders as a group was false.

Finally, the modern company is not a nexus of contracts (Eisenberg, 1989) and is not purely a creature of private law. Shareholder primacy is based on an understanding of the company as contractually based. In a shareholder primacy conception, rather than being regarded as the primary characteristic of the company, a corporate legal personality is relegated to no more than a convenient heuristic formula, a type of collective noun that describes a combination of characteristics (Watson, 2018). A modern company cannot exist without undergoing a process of incorporation set down by the state in a statute. The instant before that process is complete, the company is not a legal person; the instance after the process is completed, the company is a legal person. Another consequence of the seminal corporate law case *Salomon* v. *Salomon & Co Ltd* (1897 AC (1897)) was the determination that it is the process of incorporation meeting the requirements in the incorporation statute, not the association of shareholders, that causes the company to become a legal person. Corporate legal personality, the defining and primary characteristic of the company, is not contractually derived and could not be replicated through contracting. Comprehensive limited liability has a statutory basis.

3.2 Company as an Entity

Corporate law cannot be explained in a pure system of private ordering, even though it provides the parties with considerable flexibility (in theory) as to how the company is organised (Moore, 2014). It was the development of incorporation by registration in the mid-nineteenth century that resulted in the existence of a company not being directly dependent on an association of shareholders (Watson, 2015). One consequence is that the legal personality of the corporation needs to be central to the economic analysis of the corporation (Deakin et al., 2017). Company law involves significant mandatory statutory rules, which embody policy choices. Neither true agreement nor hypothetical bargaining can alone provide legitimacy for the decision-making within a public corporation.

Companies would not be separate legal entities and legal persons if it were not for a statute. Nor would they have comprehensive limited liability.[3] An explanation of the origins and central significance of status as a legal person in the history of the joint stock company strengthens arguments that corporate legal personality cannot be explained away as an instance of contracting and thus of private ordering (Moore, 2014). The key point is that the modern company is a hybrid. It is not wholly private, as its two key characteristics – limited liability and separate legal personality – provide it with enormous advantages by allowing for the aggregation of capital and strong form asset partitioning (including the extraction of value from its persona). The statute does not perform a gap-filling function (Kraakman et al., 2017) but rather is key to the existence of the company.

---

[3] Companies do not need to be incorporated to contract for limited liability, but they could not contract for limited liability with involuntary creditors such as tort victims of the company.

Our stance is that shareholder primacy is based on a model of the company that was legally superseded by the end of the nineteenth century. From the onset of the joint stock company in the sixteenth century, the joint stock fund was separate for accounting purposes from stockholders, a consequence of double entry bookkeeping. Accounting separation made aggregation of capitals in the fund possible. Separation and aggregation were the characteristic of the joint stock company that was sought after by entrepreneurs from Elizabethan times onwards. The introduction of limited liability in the second half of the nineteenth century saw a gradual and corresponding legal separation of the corporate fund from shareholders. That legal separation was driven in part by the development of the capital maintenance rules that protected the corporate capital fund from shareholders. That legal separation of shareholders from the company was unequivocally recognised in *Salomon* v. *Salomon & Co Ltd* (1897 AC (1897)), the seminal corporate law case, where, among other things, the House of Lords stated that interpretation of the Companies Act 1862 meant that, on formation, the company was a separate legal person from the shareholders. From that point onwards, correctly understood, shareholders were no longer legally part of the corporate legal entity, (although shareholders collectively act as an organ of the company, as discussed later).

Our shared conception of the modern company is of an entity that is a legal person. This legal person is not comprised of people but rather of a capital fund. That capital fund has the status of a legal person. The company as a legal person has a persona that enables it to capture the more intangible forms of value related to aspects like brand, reputation and goodwill. This conception of the modern company coincides with the understanding that underpins integrated reporting. Integrated reporting is a process of applying principles and concepts to improve the quality of information available for more efficient and productive allocation of capital used by business to create value over time (International Integrated Reporting Council, 2018). The capital used by business is stocks of value that are affected or transformed by the activities and outputs of an organisation, categorised as financial, manufactured, intellectual, human, social and relationship, and natural.

The legal person containing the capital fund has two decision-making organs or bodies that animate it. One organ is the general meeting (the shareholders operating collectively) and the other organ is the board (comprised of those individuals occupying the position of director). The two decision-making organs are responsible for different types of decisions on different matters. The shareholders collectively, through the general meeting, operate behind 'the corporate veil' with responsibility for 'rules of the game' decisions about the constitution of the company, the composition of the board and, in some jurisdictions, approval of major transactions and ratification rights over some decisions made by the board outside its powers. The board is responsible for decisions about the direction and management of the company, broadly defined. It is the board that steps through the veil by acting as the representative of the legal person in the world either itself or through corporate agents interacting with other corporate participants and inducing firm-specific investments (Blair & Stout, 2001). The board sits at the nexus of corporate participants.

Our model therefore places the board at the nexus of the corporate participants who interact with the company as it operates in the world, balancing at any time the interests of different stakeholders. We, however, differ from many stakeholder theorists because we recognise the importance of shareholders when they act collectively through the general meeting as an organ of the company. But it need not necessarily follow that shareholder wealth maximisation is the purpose or objective of the corporation. Instead, the role of the board is to act in the interests of the entity itself; the legal person holding or comprised of a fund comprising different types of capital.

For corporate law and governance, we argue for a shift in perspective from attempts to solve perceived agency problems between shareholders and managers to a focus on influence and control. Such an eversion in perspective would shift primarily to the board as the corporate organ normatively responsible for determining the direction of the company. The aggregation of wealth in the corporate fund means that corporate participants may seek to influence and control the entity. As well as representing the company, the board has the role of acting as the guardian of the inanimate corporate legal person that is a fund.

4 The Role of People in the Legal Person

This section begins with the identification of some of the salient features of leadership. It then briefly reviews how the economic theory of the corporation might accommodate a role for leadership. The remainder of the section is structured around the role of the board.

Three general ideas underpin this Element. First, subject to its constitution, the business of a corporation is to be managed by or to be under the direction of the board of directors. Second, competent board leadership is recognised as essential for a well-functioning system of corporate governance (Huse, 2007; Lorsch & MacIver, 1989). Third, a critical attribute of a high-performing corporate board is its ability to act as a team (Conger & Lawler, 2009a; Huse & Gabrielsson, 2012).

Board leadership has, however, not overtly played a significant role in corporate law theory.[4] While, formally, much ultimate decision-making power and responsibility within a corporation rests with the board, corporate govern- ance theory has tended to assign to the board the relatively modest role of monitoring management for equity investors. Defying everyday facts and the current preoccupation with institutional investors, some strains of corporate law theory go further to suggest that shareholders should not, and rationally would not, be involved in such decisions (see, for example, Easterbrook & Fischel, 1996). This view of board leadership is also influenced by information asym- metries between individual board members, managers and shareholders, which constrain the power of the board and may result in inefficient decision-making and ineffective performance.

In practice, the board processes behind major corporate decisions are not infrequently political. Individual shareholder and management interests may not be aligned with the goal of shareholder wealth maximisation, or there may be disagreement on how best to achieve that objective. Competing interests and objectives need to be balanced and board leadership may be critical in this context. Furthermore, decision outcomes are often negotiated or made only after extensive consultation with parties to which the contractarian view of the corporation does not give a formal decision-making role, such as creditors. Corporate boards are at the nexus of a number of relationships that constitute the corporation. The formal and informal relationships between the board and shareholders and between the board and senior management are core, but, in many cases, the board will also be at least in dialogue with company creditors, customers, suppliers and employees, as well as the government and community. Such consultation and negotiations are encouraged by many corporate govern- ance guidelines and are now seen as necessary rather than optional by the board (e.g., Institute of Chartered Secretaries and Administrators & The Investment Association, 2017).

The concept of influentiality,[5] we believe, helps to explain board leadership within the context of corporate governance. Leadership generates that which governance seeks to regulate – influence (Yukl, 2013). As influence moves towards control, regulation takes on increasing importance. Corporate law both preserves space for leadership and demands governance. Influentiality is an amalgam of leadership and governance, not just leadership in governance.

---

[4] In this Element, we refer to corporate law rather than company law to indicate that the relevant legal rules extend beyond the subject matter of company law 'proper' to include aspects of securities law and regulation, listing rules as well as soft law corporate governance codes.

[5] The Oxford English Dictionary Third edition, 2009 cites as the source of the word T. Carlyle's (1841) *Heroes*: 'Keep your red-tape clerks, your influentialities, your important businesses'.

Leadership, or influence, may flow both in the same direction and against formal accountabilities envisaged in traditional views of governance. The board, for example, is not infrequently able to, and expected to, exercise leadership both in relation to management and shareholders.

While the board formally delegates authority to management, the board is dependent on management for information. The confluence of these counter-vailing forces produces a zone for negotiation. Board decisions, especially where dominated by non-executive directors, are a product of the board's determination and persuasiveness rather than the pure exercise of fiat and establishment of formal systems of reporting (Bainbridge, 2003). The appointment and removal of the CEO is a primary function of the board. However, to allow the CEO and other senior management to manage the corporation effectively, the board needs to credibly commit to not meddling in management decisions, at least in the normal run of events.

By contrast, while the shareholders can in theory appoint and remove directors, information and collective action problems mean that shareholders will only sometimes be able to control appointments. The ability to control appointments usually coincides with a shareholder acquiring a significant parcel of shares. In the classic Berle and Means corporation, individual shareholders with small parcels of shares have little or no influence. With the presence of substantial and institutional shareholders, collective action becomes more credible. The board needs to communicate with and 'manage' the relationship with the shareholders.

The board, and the chair of the board in particular, is at the centre of a number of fundamental relationships within the corporation. From our perspective, the board must intermediate between the shareholders, management and other stakeholders. The board does so by providing leadership within each of these three domains. This view might be seen as drawing on the economic theory of the board as a mediating hierarchy (Blair & Stout, 1999), but team production theory talks about the value of the board mediating between interest groups, but does not explain how this happens (Vandewaerde et al., 2011). In addition, team production theory considers the company from the perspectives of its stakeholders, the team, rather than from the perspective of the corporate entity itself. Team production theory is fundamentally a theory about optimisation within a contractarian framework, rather than a process involving interacting with a central nexus with a role for leadership for the board. It also does not account sufficiently for the significance of shareholders within the corporate structure, in particular for the possibility that shareholders can vote to remove directors, and shareholders with a substantial but minority shareholding often have the influence to secure the appointment of one or more directors, thereby exercising direct influence over board decision-making.

The concept of a mediating hierarchy is not an accurate portrayal of the board, in the sense that the words risk implying that the board may be a passive referee exercising Solomonic judgement between competing interests. Notwithstanding its formal authority to do so, as suggested earlier, it is not correct to see the board as simply able to make major decisions without direct reference to management and shareholders. The scope for leadership and how leadership may be manifested by the board depends on the circumstances of each company, including the distribution of share ownership, the constitution of the board and the competency of the management. We see the board able to exercise leadership in an active way in its relationships with management, shareholders and other stakeholder groups, as well as in relation to its own operation.

In each of these relationships, the board can be either passive or active. Boards can actively engage with each of these groups, or they can be influenced or even controlled by one or more of these groups. This influence takes place against the background of more formal legal structures and governance structures, but the legal and formal basis of these relationship will not necessarily determine the influence or control that the constituent groups may exercise. The nature of the relationships that the board has with these groups and the extent to which the relationships external to the board are dynamic (driven by the board itself) or passive (driven by the other groups) are affected by, and impact, the internal operation of the board and the extent to which the board 'leads' the corporation.

The literature on board leadership has tended to examine the subject from one of two perspectives, as opposed to the context of the four types of relationship suggested in this Element. In the literature on the one hand, board leadership may refer to the strategic decision-making by a corporation, and maybe even hands-on leadership in times of crisis (see, for example, Finkelstein, Hambrick & Cannella, 2009; Huse & Zattoni, 2008; Lorsch, 2009; McNulty et al., 2011; Pugliese et al., 2009; Stiles & Taylor, 2001). On the other hand, leadership may refer to the leadership within the board and individual directors, in particular the chair and committee chairs (see, for example, Huse, 2005; Kakabadse, Kakabadse & Barratt, 2006; Leblanc & Gillies, 2005; Levrau & van den Berghe, 2013; Roberts, McNulty & Stiles, 2005; Roberts & Stiles, 1999).

4.1 What is Leadership?

Gary Yukl (2013) defines leadership as 'the process of influencing others to understand and agree about needs to be done and how to do it, and the process of facilitating individual and collective efforts to accomplish shared objectives'

(p. 8). It is a useful point of departure and some key features of this definition should be noted. First, leadership involves both role specialisation as well as social influence processes (Cartwright, 1965). Under the former conceptualisation, all groups are viewed as having role specialisation that includes a leadership role with some responsibilities and functions that cannot be shared too widely without jeopardising the effectiveness of the group. Under the latter, leadership is seen as a social process or pattern. While some role specialisation will occur within organisations, leadership may be shared or distributed, and there might not always be a clear distinction between leaders and followers.

Second, leadership includes both emotive and rational processes. Under the latter, followers follow because of the various rewards and punishments that the leader has available to motivate or coerce. Neither charismatic nor unethical leadership are excluded, but these qualities do not define leadership. Leaders can influence the conduct of a group in many different ways, including through the interpretation of external events for members; the choice of objectives and strategies to pursue; the motivation of members to achieve the objectives; the mutual trust and cooperation of members; the organisation and coordination of work activities; the allocation of resources to activities and objectives; the development of member skills and confidence; the learning and sharing of new knowledge by members; the enlistment of support and cooperation from outsiders; the design of formal structure, programmes and systems; and the shared beliefs and values of members (Yukl, 2013).

Third, leadership is about the process of influence (Bass & Riggio, 2006; Yukl, 2013). A number of contemporary writers, while retaining the ideas of a relationship and influence, no longer see the process as one-way but rather leadership as the product of co-production (Pearce & Conger, 2003; Rost, 1993). The process need not result in a 'successful' outcome, such as the maximisation of shareholder value. Whether an outcome is successful will depend on the perspective of the observer. The analytical separation of the process of influence from how leadership affects outcomes prevents the artificial restriction of both the definition of leadership and, in the context of this Element, the conceptualisation of the corporation.

Fourth, the concepts of followers and subordinates are distinct. Leadership processes can occur even in the absence of a formal authority relationship. The difference between leadership and management has been controversial. Most researchers agree that successful management within a complex organisation involves leadership. When significant decisions are made by an organisation to make changes within that organisation, authority as the formal power legitimately acquired based on one's role (French & Raven, 1959) is unlikely to be a sufficient basis for gaining the commitment of subordinates or for influencing other people whose cooperation is necessary, such as peers or outsiders (Anderson & Sun, 2017; Huxham & Vangen, 2000; Wang et al., 2011).

Leadership scholarship is diverse, and the subject defies easy conceptualisation. Scholars with a breadth of interests, theoretical traditions and methodological approaches have been drawn to studying leadership, contributing to the richness of the research on both the theoretical and empirical fronts and resulting in the increased diversity and specialisation of the field (for a review, see Jackson and Parry, 2018). On the one hand, the diversity has led to a multiplicity of theories of how leaders shape organisations and systems, with overlaps creating a blurring of distinctions between concepts (see, for example, reviews of charismatic and transformational leadership by Judge and Piccolo, 2004; Knippenberg and Sitkin, 2013). On the other hand, it has also led to tighter definitions and the isolation of issues, such as the concentration on outcomes of leadership rather than processes affecting the emergence of outcomes (Dinh et al., 2014; Langley et al., 2013).

Transformational leadership, one of the most widely studied contemporary leadership theories (Dinh et al., 2014; Gardner et al., 2010), brought to the fore leadership enacted at the individual, group and organisational level to create commitment and enhanced (superior) performance. In conceptualising leadership as a process, researchers see leadership as not restricted to an individual in a group who has a formal position of power (Bass et al., 2003). Leadership, as a process, takes place between leaders and followers towards the achievement of a desired end point or towards a goal to be realised together. The effect of transformational leadership goes well beyond the quid pro quo approach of contingent social and economic rewards and sanctions of transactional leadership. It accommodates aspects of leadership that are positively oriented and associated with good outcomes as well as those negatively oriented aspects linked with destructive outcomes (Bass & Steidlmeier, 1999; Schyns & Schilling, 2013; Tourish, 2013).

More recently, the emergence of shared or team leadership has drawn attention to the tensions between individual and collective dimensions of leadership (Jackson & Parry, 2018; Mehra et al., 2006; Pearce, Conger & Locke, 2008; Thorpe, Gold & Lawler, 2011). This approach suggests that shared leadership arises through the social interactions among team members rather than as an aggregation of the characteristics of individual team members. Team members rely on skills, knowledge and expertise to exercise individual leadership among one another to meet shared goals and objectives. In this way, leadership is dispersed rather than concentrated in the hands of one individual. Leadership, as a function or activity rather than a role, is shared among members of the group to facilitate adaptive, coordinated and integrated action/performance. Collectively, the trend towards the study of relational and team forms of leadership suggests that social context, including the emergence of shared leadership within teams, contributes insights to an improved understanding of leadership. The orientation towards contextualised theorising of leadership suggests the importance of different organisational settings and issues where leadership is understood within the demands of various roles and functions of organisations (Wilson et al., 2018).

4.2 Integrating Leadership into the Economic Analysis of the Corporation

While countless books have been written on leadership, the topic has received scant attention from economists. Reasons stem, in part, from strong assumptions about rationality and utility maximising; and multi-period models of decision-making with asymmetric information quickly become complex and contain multiple equilibria (Zupan, 2010). What literature there is tends to focus on the CEO rather than the board.

A review of some of the economics literature helps to connect leadership to the economic theory that structures much of the analysis of corporate governance and corporate law, including revealing some of the limitations of the analysis. The application of economic analysis of leadership to boards provides insight into the role of the board and its treatment in corporate law.

An early model conceived the problems of leadership within an organisation as the difficulty that the leader has to motivate his or her followers within the organisation (Rotemberg & Saloner, 1993). Like the traditional principal–agent problem, Rotemberg and Saloner (1993) see the leader as having the problem of incentivising the followers to exert effort to improve the firm's overall performance. In their model, the very fact that an improvement might be fully evaluated and taken into account is a sufficient incentive for followers to make suggestions. Inspired by *kaizen* (or continual improvement), the leader's problem is to credibly commit to being a good listener and communicator, which can be solved if the leader has the welfare of the whole organisation at heart.

Based on the private information that the leader has about the return of effort for the team as a whole, Hermalin's model shows that self-interested agents can be motivated by a leader exerting high effort (Hermalin, 1998). Leading by example makes credible the leader's belief in what he or she is doing. The model has been extended to a repeated game context and a team setting (Hermalin, 2007; Huck & Rey-Biel, 2006). This, and other models based on information (e.g., Kobayashi & Suehiro, 2005), seems less relevant to a board's relationship to management, where non-executive directors are almost always at a significant information disadvantage relative to management, but perhaps not to shareholders.

Where followers would like to coordinate but cannot because they do not know what others believe, the leader can communicate information that facilitates coordination (Dewan & Myatt, 2008; Ferreira & Rezende, 2007). Building on the prisoner's dilemma, Zupan (2010) argues that leadership can be understood from an economic perspective as moving people stuck in an inferior equilibrium of the game (a one-shot game) into a superior equilibrium (an indefinitely repeated game). Many of the commonly cited requirements for good leadership can, he claims, be accommodated.

Behavioural characteristics of individuals matter. The finance literature has examined how overconfident executives can attract and motivate followers and win tournaments (Gervais & Goldstein, 2007; Goel & Thakor, 2008; Steen, 2005). The overconfidence of CEOs has been viewed by some as problematic, especially in a post-financial crisis environment. In these circumstances, the board has a role in critically evaluating significant proposed management initiatives.

Bolton, Brunnermeier and Veldkamp (2010, 2012), building on the principal–agent framework, present an economic model of leadership that specifies an organisational leader's challenge as credibly communicating a mission that enables coordinated actions by followers in the face of potential changes. The problem can be partially solved by the appointment of a leader known for his or her resoluteness, which was interpreted as the leader sticking to the decided course even when he or she would rationally change course in light of subsequent information. The implication is that the leader's behavioural traits and interaction with followers are important determinants of a corporation's performance.

Bolton and colleagues (Bolton, Brunnermeier and Veldkamp, 2012) speculated that a board may appoint different types of leaders at different stages in a firm's life cycle. At times, a more resolute leader able to foster greater coordination may be critical. Our study of the successive appointment of an airline's CEOs could be interpreted in this light (Cikaliuk et al., 2018a).

Further implications are that the resoluteness of the board may affect the continuing tenure or compensation of the CEO. The same issue of time inconsistency that can affect the CEO can also affect the board, raising questions about the role of the board in formulating as opposed to reviewing strategy. Director primacy, in the form of decision by fiat, may also not be without its costs. The resoluteness of the board can be enhanced by controlling changes in board membership and making decisions by consensus.

The economic literature is seeking to capture some of the factors that have long been features of the management literature, but little evidence of predictive power or correlation with improved performance has been uncovered.

While economic theory recognised a role for the CEO to motivate, communicate, coordinate and commit, it does not capture the complexity of the relationships within an organisation. It does not, for example, address the potential role of the board in coordinating between management and shareholders, and perhaps other stakeholders, simultaneously. The attempt to explain all of corporate governance with economic models risks significantly truncating the richer and more complex mechanisms appreciated by corporate law and management.

4.3 The Role of the Board through the Lens of Leadership

If corporate governance theory is a rigid box, leadership is a shapeless and ghost-like presence. Despite the wealth of scholarly attention devoted to leadership in organisations and leadership of organisations, a focus on the role of the board from a leadership perspective has been slow to emerge (Erakovic & Jackson, 2012). This may be due, in part, to the sense that the highest and best use of the board was a monitoring role. The dominance of the principal–agent issue limited the focus of the board's role to oversight of the performance of the executive office and the selection and dismissal of the CEO. Subsequent theoretical and empirical contributions have made evident the limitations and partiality of explanations of the board's leadership role in the absence of actual board behaviour (Huse, 2005, 2007; Pettigrew & McNulty, 1995). In seeking to expand an understanding of the board's role beyond monitoring, Zahra and Pearce (1989) and Pettigrew (1992) were among the early scholars who encouraged researchers to engage with directors and governance contexts as much remained to be learned about behaviours, relationships and effects.

Scholars coming from different research traditions have been drawn to this opportunity and viewed the role of the board through different lenses, reflecting their different backgrounds. Collectively, boards are expected to perform their role and to perform it well. However, uncertainties about the effects of boards has generated a type of haziness that is very much associated with different understandings of precisely what is the role of the board from a leadership perspective. This is, by no means, a deficiency as it provides opportunity for scholars to learn more about the nature of the board's role from a leadership lens through investigation.

One such study has linked leadership to the practice of governance in three modes: fiduciary, strategy and generative (Chait, Ryan & Taylor, 2005). The fiduciary mode encompasses the traditional/conventional aspects of oversight of management and assets. The strategic mode involves a partnership/collaborative approach with management to shape the future viability and sustainability of the organisation. The generative mode features relationships of trust with others to bring about transformational change.

The distinction is that the fiduciary and strategy modes utilise and leverage the resource base whereas the generative mode provides an opportunity for leadership to be enacted. The generative mode subsumes the fiduciary and strategy modes. In the generative mode, leadership can be exercised, in part, because there is a relationship among the directors and with the CEO. These relationships, not just a linkage, leave room for ambiguity, adaptability and interdependence to affect the performance of the board.

This suggests that boards are more than a collection of talented individuals operating in isolation; boards involve collaboration and cooperation. Effort needs to be directed at the continuous development and refinement of processes that enable boards to leverage knowledge, skills and know-how in order to create hospitable environments to bring about effective board dynamics. In this way, boards operate as teams in accumulating and sharing knowledge to enhance a company's value-creating activities. A team leadership perspective is particularly appropriate for understanding the role of the board as a locus of decision-making as it involves understanding what is going on between people. The emergence of team leadership within a board is facilitated by a boardroom culture that supports the collective contribution of each director in aiding the board to realise its designated role. Although the composition of the board changes over time as individual directors are elected and subsequently retire from the board, leadership continues to be enacted by the board. In this way, as a collective entity, the board itself demonstrates leadership.

Huse, who has produced a series of influential works and books (Huse, 2005, 2007), set the agenda for subsequent investigations of the board's role to operate as a team. Key ideas expounded include the board's role in affecting organisational outcomes through collective or joint efforts as a group rather than as a collection of disparate directors with skills and knowledge elected or appointed to the board. This has directed attention to how boards accomplish their tasks through relationships within the boardroom and beyond which emphasise collective efforts, regardless of formal role (Ees, Gabrielsson & Huse, 2009; Machold et al., 2011; Minichilli et al., 2012).

The processes and mechanisms for enacting the role of the board are allied with leadership concepts which include the role of the board chair. There is widespread acceptance among those who examine board leadership dynamics that the role of the chairperson is central and critical (Carter & Lorsch, 2004; Huse, 2009; Leblanc, 2005; McNulty et al., 2011). The board chair's role is influenced, in part, by the monitoring aspect and the functioning of the board as a whole. In fulfilling their role, board chairs engage in leadership to build relationships within the board and external to the board and to achieve the tasks/responsibilities aspect of the board's role. Previous work has identified the board chair's role in terms of value creation. Huse (2009) identified tasks undertaken by board chairs for value creation, including to build trustful relationships among board members and with the CEO; to support the board members to become effective team members by motivating and providing them with all of the information that they might need; to encourage open communications within and outside the boardroom; to facilitate robust discussions at the meetings; and to actively develop and refine governance structures and processes.

Research on trait theories (which includes demographics as a category), leadership skill and competence, and leadership style (including transformational and transactional leadership) has begun to explore the role of board chairs. There is a small but growing body of research on gender and board chairs (Cikaliuk et al., 2018b), the decision-making style of board chairs (Levrau & van den Berghe, 2013) and the attributes of an effective board chair (Huse, 2009; Kakabadse, Kakabadse & Barratt, 2006). Others have examined the role of the board chair in relation to CEOs and building a trust-based working relationship among directors (Gabrielsson, Huse & Minichilli, 2007).

Another leadership concept that is particularly useful is transactional leadership. Transactional leadership focuses on the more conventional and widely recognised hierarchical relationship between the board and CEO. In the prototypical version of this form of leadership, reward-based transactions (or exchanges) that occur among leaders (such as the board) and CEO are emphasised.

Transactional leadership is most closely allied with the principal–agent relationship in which monitoring and oversight occurs and outcomes are specified, such as a contract for the CEO (Eisenhardt, 1989). It is here that agency theory and transactional leadership appear to align in addressing perceived CEO self-interest and the attempt to motivate behaviours through the promise of reward. In the exchange, which is based on a discussion with the CEO to identify what is required (goal achievement), conditions are specified and rewards identified that will be allocated if the requirements are fulfilled (contingent reward). In this way, transactional leadership enacted between the board and CEO results in CEOs fulfilling their end of the deal by meeting performance targets and they are rewarded accordingly (Judge and Piccolo, 2004). It is here that another key role of the board chair emerges – that of mediator (Gabrielsson, Huse & Minichilli, 2007; Roberts & Stiles, 1999). The board chair smooths relations among sceptical directors, procures resources and provides inspiration when problems appear to be insurmountable.

In situations where the board of directors is oriented towards monitoring and controlling roles, the CEO will align her/his orientation with the board and avoid risk-taking behaviours. This type of board/CEO leadership promotes short-term performance in which the CEO is rewarded for incremental change which allows companies to earn a living in the present. In other words, the board/CEO leads the company in doing what they do, but better. This type of board/CEO relationship tends to support organisational exploitation rather than exploration (March, 1991). Exploitation promotes governance practices (and forms of governance) which are linked to an established strategy and strategic decision-making operates to support preservation of current organisational legitimacy (Kraatz & Block, 2008). The challenge is for boards/CEOs to find ways to retain characteristics of exploitation (short-term goals, improvements of existing capabilities and resources, repetition, systematic reasoning, coordinating activities, monitoring) and exploration (long-term vision, development of new strategies, risk-taking behaviour, mentoring, creativity) and dynamically balance them. Too little exploration may be as detrimental to the company's long-term survival as too much.

Another leadership concept is relevant – co-leadership. Heenan and Bennis (1999) coined the term and defined co-leadership as two leaders in vertically contiguous positions who share the responsibilities of leadership and are truly exceptional deputies. Although 'we continue to be mesmerized by celebrity and preoccupied with being No. 1', this tends to overestimate the value of the contributions of the chair or CEO and undervalues those made by many different people in the organisation (Heenan & Bennis, 1999, p. 6). This approach recognises that, as companies expand and diversify, it becomes increasingly more difficult for one person to have the skills, knowledge and experience to lead organisations in realising their full value-creating potential (O'Toole, Galbraith & Lawler, 2002). As Heenan and Bennis (1999, p. viii) pointed out, 'The genius of our age is truly collaborative' and 'the shrewd leaders of the future are those who recognize the significance of creating alliances with others whose fates are correlated with their own'. When it comes to leadership, a two-in-the-box model may engender strengthened performance in the long term.

Co-leadership reinforces a conception that leadership is not a solitary activity; it thrives on collaboration. Despite limited rigorous analysis, several scholars have suggested that it improves leadership effectiveness (Alvarez & Svejenova, 2005; Heenan & Bennis, 1999; O'Toole, Galbraith & Lawler, 2002; Sally, 2002). Hambrick and Mason (1984) theorised that the perceptions of senior executives, that is, their experiences, values and personalities, are highly influential in how companies respond to and cope with changes in the environment, shaping them in ways that resemble their views on strategy and risk. The upper echelons theory advanced by Hambrick and Mason (1984) proposes that organisations become reflections of the top management team's strategic choices, suggesting that the complexity of organisations make it improbable for one individual to exert great influence over all members. Other researchers, with different perspectives, similarly maintain that there is a lack of research evidence that single individuals have the kind of dramatic impact on organisational performance (Thorpe, Gold & Lawler, 2011). A formal co-leadership (i.e., co-CEO, co-chair, co-director) structure can help to make this more likely, but these remain the notable exception rather than the rule.

It is the board's leadership in strategy where its role in value creation is brought into greater focus. Through engagement with 'the business environment, relationships and the promotion of shared interests' (Freeman, 1984, p. 192), the board acts to ensure the long-term success of the company. Along with understanding the external business environment (ecosystem) within which the company operates, the board balances and integrates multiple relationships that taken together affect value creation. Such a perspective positions the board's leadership role as bringing about survival and value creation.

Forbes and Milliken (1999) were among the earliest scholars to discuss boards as strategic decision-making groups. They proposed a model that links factors with board-level outcomes, such as task performance and cohesiveness, and then relates them with firm performance. A decade later, Pugliese et al. (2009) found from their review of the literature on boards and strategy that boards are engaged in strategy. They identified the nature of boards' strategic involvement as including an active role to define it at a general level, a responsibility for specific outcomes and some level of participation in the strategy-making process.

The role of the board from a leadership lens is subject to multiple conceptual treatments. Each of these provide important insights that contribute to an understanding of the role of the board. Perhaps the most important theoretical insight emerges from a consideration of purpose. In many respects, the role of the board through a leadership lens involves ensuring the viability of the company and promoting its sustainability. Our understanding of the board's role is to add value by enacting leadership in governance.

5 The Board as a Nexus of Relationships

In this section, the integrative model is introduced. We start by examining how the board is traditionally characterised in corporate governance theory and commonly in corporate law scholarship, as well as point to some of the inadequacies of these theories. It does not claim that concerns about board leadership are, or have ever, shaped corporate law. It may, however, be possible to say that corporate law is consistent with the board exercising and coordinating influence across several domains. To put it colloquially, some play in the joints is required if leadership is to matter. The remaining part of this section examines the board at the centre or nexus of the participants who interact with and around the modern corporation. It explains how the relationships of the board with shareholders, among the directors, management and non-shareholding stakeholders, position the board to normatively govern and lead the company. We elaborate on aspects of organisational studies and legal disciplinary insights which inform the integrative model and new directions evoked for scholars and practitioners to pursue.

5.1 Towards an Integrative Model

The primary role of the board normatively is to act in the best interests of the corporate legal entity, which is a legal or juridical person. The board is also charged with safeguarding the corporate legal entity. In doing so, the board should protect the corporate fund as well as the other forms of value which the company acquires and generates as it operates in the world.

The ability of corporate boards to take account of the interests of the employees, environment and local community when seeking to act in the interests of the company as a whole is now widely accepted. The limited reviewability of board decisions creates further scope for the board to bargain with stakeholder groups and the ability of stakeholder groups to pressure the board to bargain.

The directors who comprise the board are therefore a collective charged with complex decision-making (Lorsch & Clark, 2008). The board will engage with corporate participants or stakeholders that interact with the company. At the same time, the board must ensure that the influence over decision-making by corporate participants does not morph into control by those participants.

The relationship between the board and shareholders is complex and differs from any of the other relationships that the board has with other corporate participants. The founding shareholders come together to form the company. On incorporation, a separate juridical entity or legal person is created that owns or controls the corporate fund. The founding shareholders specify, in the constitution, articles of incorporation or equivalent, the procedures which will be followed to operate the venture. The existence of a default constitution or equivalent solves the problem of incomplete contracting for shareholders as initial participants (Robé, 2011). In return, shareholders are issued shares. Although the company as a legal person owns the corporate fund, shareholders own shares.

Those shares typically have rights attached to them. The rights include in personam rights for shareholders such as the right to receive notice of and participate in shareholder meetings as part of one of the decision-making organs of the company. Rights also attach to the shares and might be called capital rights. Examples of capital rights are entitlements to pro rata shares of dividends and residual rights on dissolution. Those rights affect shareholders as investors. Shareholders also usually have voting rights on the election of board members. It is now common for voting rights to be attached to shares rather than persons. In practice, this right affects the number of votes each shareholder has (a shareholder will vote all of his/her or its votes in the same way). But shareholders are also stakeholders; like all stakeholders, some shareholders individually or in groups will seek to influence decision-making by boards. The potential ability of shareholders through participation in the corporate organ of the company, the meeting, or the voting to appoint or remove directors from the board means that the influence of shareholders with big voting blocs may be great. That does not mean that the shareholders own the company; rather, through the voting rights attached to their shares, they have the potential to influence or even control the board. And as discussed in Section 3.2, the shareholding organ, the meeting, has some decision-making rights.

The recognition that no single body is in charge of all decisions as well as the non-contractual side to corporate law suggests that the legal structure of the company cannot in theory be guaranteed to lead to the maximisation of shareholder wealth. The neoclassical assumptions underpinning the principal–agent approach to corporation law have been under sustained attack for several decades from behavioural theorists that have shown that much behaviour can be explained through the concepts of bounded rationality, satisficing, the routinisation of decision-making in standard operating procedures and the dominant coalition. Leadership could play a positive or negative role within such an environment.

Positively, leadership can, for example, reduce the satisficing behaviour of individual managers or directors. This is consistent with the fairly basic economic models of the motivational role of a leader.

Two implications arise from the multitude of reasons why corporate directors, managers and shareholders might not be relentlessly focused on a common vision of shareholder wealth maximising. First, there might be a diversity of actors, with a diversity of objectives within the company. Second, where control is not absolute, that is, where both director and shareholder primacy are missing, corporate decisions will be negotiated. In any event, conceptions of shareholder wealth maximisation and associated time horizons are likely to differ between directors, managers and shareholders.

Drawing a slightly longer bow, a further implication is that simple rules, derived from the property-based fiduciary duties of directors, such as the duty not to profit from office and the duty to avoid conflicts of interest, ostensibly aimed at protecting shareholder wealth, are an insufficient basis for a system of corporate governance. Arguably, not all fiduciary duties can be contracted out (Lim, 2015). The concern of the law is to regulate the conduct of shareholders as well as directors where shareholders misuse power. Courts and legislatures will not permit shareholders that hold the majority of shares to act unconscionably towards minority-interest shareholders.

In listed companies, day-to-day management is delegated by the board to senior executives. The information acquired by executives and their day-to-day involvement with the operation of the company creates potential information asymmetries between the board and executive management that have been recognised by the literature. Less often identified but discussed in this Element is the consequential potential influence and control by management.

Companies will also have employees. Much economic literature treats the relationship between the company and employees as based on contract. Although employees collectively are not an organ of the company, employees, together with management, contribute human capital or value to the company. Although not measurable in the same way as financial capital, human capital is part of the value of a corporate legal entity. Human capital is used to generate value for the company that can be converted to financial capital. Many civil law jurisdictions, most notably Germany, recognise the significance of employees to the company by allowing employee representation on the supervisory board of the company. Such representation is also recognition of the impact of the company on employees. In common law jurisdictions, employee representation on boards is not common, although the British prime minister Theresa May did suggest employee representation when she was made prime minister (Baker, 2016). Intermediate steps such as employee committees that meet with boards have been mooted. Such initiatives are instances of boards interacting with a stakeholder group.

Shareholders have a number of relationships with the company. As well as shares giving individual rights to shareholders to act through the general meeting as an organ of the company, shareholders are also investors. Accumulation of blocs of shares by major shareholders, the rise of socially responsible investment and increasingly active institutional investors like BlackRock mean that boards meet with investor groups.

Beyond the identified stakeholders, companies operate in a world where, at any time, a moving and changing web of stakeholders will either be affected by the company or will affect the company. An active board will interact with the moving and changing stakeholder groups. Those stakeholder groups may legitimately collude with each other to influence the board and therefore the company. An example might be environmental bodies joining with regulatory bodies to encourage sustainable behaviour by a company. Sometimes stakeholder interests may not align. An example might be a sustainable environmental initiative that may result in loss of jobs by employees. The role of the board is not to mediate between interest groups that may be in conflict – we do not consider the board to be a mediating hierarchy (Blair & Stout, 1999). Instead, the role of the board is to make decisions that are in the interests of the corporate legal person and the corporate legal entity. But as well as making the best decision possible for the company at any time, the board, when acting in the long-term interests of the company, must ensure that its relationships with stakeholder groups are maintained.

Increasingly the importance of board diversity is being recognised. However, with diversity comes a range of world views that may result in differences of opinion about the direction a company should take. In addition, nominee directors appointed by shareholders may advocate for a direction that benefits the nominator. The extent to which members of the board should be representative of corporate constituents and the extent to which members of the board should be independent remain contested.

5.2 The Board and Shareholders

While never quite able to monopolise the field, for many years, agency theory has been the dominant paradigm in the practice and study of corporate governance. In their review of academic journal articles on board leadership, Yar Hamidi and Gabrielsson (2014a) found that the research predominantly investigated CEO/chair duality, focused on publicly listed companies, used a quantitative methodology and archival data, relied strongly on agency theory, and was mainly based on US data. Within this paradigm, the directors and senior management on the board are seen as agents of the shareholders. Corporate law and governance practices are intended to align the incentives of managerial agents with the interest of shareholders as the principal also deterring opportunistic behaviour by the board and management. A distinction is also drawn between management and the governance role of the board.

The legitimacy and desirability of contractarian models are built on the notions of individual rationality and agreement (Moore, 2014). While shareholders are the residual risk bearers (at least while the corporation remains solvent) and collectively have the power to appoint the directors, contractarianism does not expect shareholders to be active participants in corporate governance (Easterbrook & Fischel, 1996). Indeed, it is generally suspicious of any exercises of shareholder voting power. The informational and collective action impediments to the effective functioning of the shareholder franchise within large public corporations with widely dispersed shareholdings are indeed significant.

If shareholders were actually the simple rational maximisers that they are assumed to be, there would be limited need for active board engagement with shareholders, at least beyond communications from the board to the shareholders. If a diversified portfolio is the only practical option open to shareholders to protect their interests, due to informational and collective action problems, there would be no scope or need for the board to exercise leadership in relation to shareholders. While shareholder passivity is presented by contractarians as a virtue, empirical evidence demonstrates that shareholders are not always passive.

These ideas are helpful in charting the relationship between the board and shareholders. Despite the formal authority that shareholders may possess, and the legitimate concerns about lax or opportunistic behaviour of management, some boards are able to exercise leadership in their relations with shareholders. Statutorily mandated communication between the board and the shareholders, such as annual meetings and reports, are not simply compliance activities, nor perhaps even primarily a means of ensuring board accountability to shareholders. Two-way communication between the board and shareholders can help tame shareholder activism, garner additional resources for the company, and more generally build greater trust between the company and its longer-term shareholders.

Enhanced levels of shareholder communication and engagement have been witnessed in a number of jurisdictions, notably the UK and the United States, and has become an established part of conventional good governance recommendations (Aguilar, 2015). Several reasons for increased shareholder engagement have been suggested, including say-on-pay legislation, influence of proxy advisory firms and concentration of share ownership, in particular in the hands of institutional investors.

The legal framework provides space, albeit imperfectly, for this model of leadership in governance to operate. The shareholders as a group have formal powers to elect directors and approve a few significant corporate decisions. Nonetheless, a set of rules can be identified that protect the space for the board to act as leaders.

The topic of insulated boards has generated considerable discussion in the United States (Bebchuk, 2013; Strine, 2014). Corporate law writings and debates question claims that insulating or shielding boards from share-holder pressure by limiting their rights and powers serves the long-term interests of publicly traded companies and their long-term shareholders. The centre of gravity within the discussion differs from the usual position under Anglo-Australasian law where shareholders have generally had greater control, de jure or de facto, over corporate boards. The listing requirements now provide for a minimum number of independent directors. The rules also recognise that directors may (at least initially) be appointed by other directors. The board has influence over the future constitution of the board. With limited exceptions, nominee directors have a duty to act in the interests of the company and not their appointor and a duty not to fetter their discretion.

Of the boards we have studied, the board of an airline perhaps come closest to the ideal of the insulated board. Notwithstanding the government owning approximately 80 per cent of the shares, successive shareholding ministers left the board alone to make strategic decisions for the company (see Section 6.3).

The discretion of the board is also protected by the same rules that protect minority shareholders. The unfair prejudice remedy and the derivative action protect the board from being subject to the demands of majority shareholders. It appears that shareholders – even acting unanimously – do not have the power to usurp the decision-making role allocated to directors in the corporate constitution. Furthermore, the business decisions of the board are not subject to review by the courts (*Howard Smith Ltd* v. *Ampol Petroleum Ltd*, 1974 AC (1974)). The deference to the board's business decisions is also reflected in the nature of the obligations imposed on directors. For example, the unfair prejudice remedy has been interpreted to preclude complaints about decisions that can be attributed to business judgement. The fiduciary duties of directors are intended to ensure directors work zealously for the company, but strict rules dealing with conflicts of interest and accounts of profits do invite the courts to make business judgements, including on whether a company could have taken advantage of a business opportunity (*Fhr European Ventures Llp* v. *Cedar Capital Partners LLC*, 2014 UKSC (2014)).

Whether the duty of loyalty is seen as a fiduciary duty or a separate duty reinforced by fiduciary duties, loyalty is primarily assessed as a subjective duty (*In re Smith and Fawcett Ltd*, 1942 Ch. (1942)). Where elements of objectivity have crept into the duty, particularly in cases involving corporate groups and passive-follower directors, the duty has been articulated in procedural terms. The question the courts have asked is: did the director consider the interests of the company?

5.3 Within the Board

In an era of accelerating economic and technological change, boards that merely react to events cannot hope to be effective. Boards must work to foresee the challenges and opportunities that their companies face. Many experts advise that boards need to think deeply about the business, bringing new ideas and analysis to the table, engage in long-term strategic planning, and be prepared to challenge the status quo and catalyse change when necessary (Dailey & Koblentz, 2012). For this to occur, the board must not only have the appropriate skills, experience and judgement, but also the requisite leadership and governance.

From this perspective, discussions of term limits and diversity of board members are elements of a broader task of reviewing the performance of the board. The board may show leadership in relation to its own make up and decision-making processes. Having the 'right' people is part of this. But there will also be trade-offs that need to be made, between skills and diversity and representation of shareholders.

While investors more or less systematically review the performance of boards, as discussed earlier, the influence of shareholders is often by design or in practice significantly attenuated. The board frequently has influence over directorial appointments. The performance of the board is therefore a matter that the board itself needs to periodically review. The review needs to encompass the board's composition, leadership, interpersonal dynamics, governance policies, strategic vision and so on (Institute of Corporate Directors, Canada, 2015). Virtually all S&P 500 companies have established a framework for evaluating their performance as a group, but only about a third evaluate the performance of individual directors (SpencerStuart, 2018).

The governance processes, both within the board and in the broader corporate environment, help to mediate between the competing objectives by providing for information gathering, monitoring, review and consultation. In a number of jurisdictions, regulation or reporting requirements have sought to promote, inter alia, diversity, directorial renewal and other restrictions on board make-up and tenure. Agency theory-based research on the effect of board structure on shareholder wealth has not produced strong results. While individually important, and increasingly addressed in listing requirements and good governance guidelines, a general review of the specific requirements is beyond the scope of the present work (for a discussion of best practice, see Conger & Lawler, 2009a).

Two issues merit specific attention in this Element because they arise from primary rather than secondary corporate law: first, leadership within the board, particularly the role of the chairperson, and second, the balance between collective action and individual responsibility.

5.3.1 Leadership and Self-governance

The legal characterisation of the corporate board in Anglo-Australasian law remains contested. Whether or not the board is correctly described as an organ of the company, the board of directors is at times a group of individuals but it is also a collective body – a team. The two sides are evident in the much-cited statement of Lord Woolf MR in *Re Westmid Packing Services Ltd, Secretary of State for Trade and Industry* v. *Griffiths:*

> [T]he collegiate or collective responsibility of the board of directors of a company is of fundamental importance to corporate governance under English company law. That collegiate or collective responsibility must however be based on individual responsibility. Each individual director owes duties to the company to inform himself about its affairs and to join with his co-directors in supervising and controlling them. (*In Re Westmid Packing Services Ltd*, 1998 All ER 2 (1998), p. 653)

The collective responsibility of the board for the long-term success of the company is the first of the main principles in the UK Corporate Governance Code (Financial Reporting Council, 2018). By contrast, directors' duties are applied to individual directors.

A similar tension is evident in the study of team leadership and shared leadership (Pearce & Sims, 2000; Yukl, 2013). While little linkage between the research on board leadership and traditional leadership research exists, interestingly, some research on shared leadership on corporate boards has been undertaken (Conger and Lawler, 2009a; Vandewaerde et al., 2011). Pearce and Conger (2003) define shared leadership as 'a dynamic, interactive influence process among individuals in groups for which the objective is to lead one another to the achievement of group or organization goals or both' and 'this influence process involves peer, or lateral, influence and at other times involves upwards or downwards hierarchical influence' (p. 1). Team leadership involves collective construction processes where the exercise of agency is practiced by individuals, shared by members of the team or both. Team leadership must also involve more than recognition that board members change from time to time. While the chair of the board often represents the board as the public face, the board acts as a collective, generally by consensus.

5.3.2 Chair of the Board

While the role of the chair is barely recognised in Anglo-Australasian company law statutes, corporate governance codes attach considerable importance to chair of the board of directors. The UK Corporate Governance Code, for example, states that the chair is responsible for the leadership of the board and for ensuring its effectiveness in all aspects of its role (Financial Reporting Council, 2018). It then elaborates on the general duty, making the chair responsible for setting the board's agenda; promoting a culture of openness and debate by facilitating the effective contribution of non-executive directors in particular; ensuring constructive relations between executive and non-executive directors; and ensuring effective communication with shareholders generally.

The responsibilities undertaken by an individual director in a company can affect the scope of his or her duty. Anglo-Australasian law might recognise additional requirements for a board chair to comply with his or her directorial duties. Duty of care for a chair may be different than that of an ordinary executive director. Similarly, members of board subcommittees that are delegated a particular function might find themselves held to a different and higher standard in relation to certain matters. These examples are still exceptions to the general rule.

The constitution of most companies provides that the chair of the board would normally also chair meetings of the board. There is, however, no requirement that the chair be 'neutral'. The chair of the board can chair a company meeting even where the matter to be discussed is the removal of all of the directors of the company, including the chair.

Notwithstanding the recent emphasis on the role of the chair of the board, the courts are clear that the board as a whole and individual directors must not allow one individual to dominate. For example, in *Madoff Securities International Ltd v. Raven* (2013 EWHC (2013)), Popplewell said that it is a breach of duty for a director 'to allow himself to be dominated, bamboozled or manipulated by a dominant fellow director' leading to a total abrogation of responsibility (p. 191). The same is true where the dominance is exercised by a subset of the directors rather than a single individual (see, for example, *Re AG (Manchester) Ltd, Official Receiver v. Watson*, 2008 EWHC (2008)). The UK Corporate Governance Code states that non-executive directors should be responsible for performance evaluation of the chair, taking into account the views of the executive directors (Financial Reporting Council, 2018).

Although law and legal literature have not sufficiently recognised the role of the chair, scholars from a behavioural perspective on boards (see, for example, Erakovic & Jackson, 2012; Kakabadse, Kakabadse & Barratt, 2006; Levrau & van den Berghe, 2013; Yar Hamidi & Gabrielsson, 2014b, among others) have explored various aspects of chair leadership. Leblanc (2005) clearly stressed the importance of the chair appointment, arguing that 'the choice of the chair of a board and the effectiveness of that chair once in that position could be considered to be the most important decision that a board of directors makes'

(p. 655). In governance practice, the chair is a director of the board as a 'peer among equals' and cannot act independently to make substantive decisions, as already emphasised by law. McNulty and colleagues (2011) maintained that there are two primary ways that a board chair can influence good collective decisions. They argue that behavioural and relational factors, along with the structural leadership position/role of the chairperson, affect the ability of the chairperson to influence decisions. Levrau and van den Berghe (2013) argued that eye-to-eye decision-making style (among others) was the preferred style of board chairs and the most effective.

The role of an effective chair can be seen as a mix of monitoring, deciding and advising in exercising the board's responsibilities (Carter & Lorsch, 2004). As Leblanc and Gillies (2005) suggested, effective chairmanship can be most closely associated with the role of 'conductor'. For the chair to be effective, she/he needs to have such attributes as presence, maturity and a sense of independence of mind along with the ability to work through tensions in achieving consensus (Kakabadse, Kakabadse & Barratt, 2006). However, the authors also noted that the 'the contribution of the chairman substantially differs from one company to the other, according to variance in context, principally company performance, and the nature of critical decisions required' (p. 141).

Effective chairs develop high-quality relationships with others (fellow directors, management, shareholders and other stakeholders) and such variance in the perception of chair leadership effectiveness may be influenced by personality qualities and characteristics such as emotional and spiritual intelligence (Harrison & Murray, 2012). In their study of board chair leadership in non-profit organisations, the authors examined and identified attributes such as being 'committed, proactive, clear about their leadership role, aware of key issues and able to see the big picture, handle conflict, and act collaboratively' as critical qualities of chairmanship (Harrison & Murray, 2012, p. 432). Another group of authors (Gabrielsson, Huse & Minichilli, 2007) argued that the attributes of an effective chair include the ability to motivate and use the competence of each board member (e.g., coach effectively and emphasise attributes of high-performance teamwork), having an open and trustful leadership style, working well together with the CEO, and continually developing the working structures and processes of the board. While these works represent perspectives from multiple disciplines outside of the mainstream leadership literature, they share the unifying theme that board chair behaviours and processes are a significant factor in board effectiveness. At the same time, leadership and governance are context dependent, suggesting that studies at the micro level of leadership and board chairs in differing contexts are desirable.

5.3.3 Group Loyalty and Individual Accountability for the Group

Loyalty of individual directors to each other and the group of directors as a whole is often a requirement for the board to be able to have a leadership role in relation to shareholders, management and other stakeholders. If the directors are unflinchingly loyal to their appointors, then the board will not be able to function as a group and lead the company. Such directors may also risk being in breach of their fundamental duty of loyalty to the company. On the other hand, if the board members were pushed too far to monitor each other's conduct, the board may struggle to form a collective identity.

Board decisions tend, in practice, to be made by consensus. Legal rules, however, push in the direction of individual accountability and the need for directors to monitor each other's behaviour. The rules governing the proceedings of the board facilitate informal decision-making by the board, while presuming any director present at a meeting of the board to have agreed to, and to have voted in favour of, a resolution of the board unless he or she expressly dissents from or votes against the resolution of the meeting. These rules are part of a scheme to provide for accountability of the board to the shareholders and creditors, and contrast with the rules that facilitate the board controlling its own proceedings, constitution and review of its performance.

An examination of when company law rules require directors to be disloyal to the directors as a collective shows how company law mediates the need for the board to demonstrate team leadership and lead the company.

A director has a duty to exercise independent judgement (*Clark v. Workman*, 1920 IR 1 (1920); Companies Act 2006). The duty does not prevent a director relying on professional advice or honestly and reasonably relying on a fellow director with greater experience or expertise. Directors may enter contracts on behalf of the company with third parties that bind them to take further action at board meetings or otherwise necessary to carry out the contract, where the decision to enter the contract was a bona fide exercise of discretion (*Fulham Football Club Ltd v. Cabra Estates Plc*, 1994 BCLC 1 (1994); *Thorby v. Goldberg*, 112 CLR (1964)). The directors, however, cannot contract to do something that is contrary to their duties to the company or the shareholders. Davies and Worthington (2008) go further, saying the starting point is that 'directors cannot validly contract (either with one another or with third parties) as to how they shall vote at future board meetings or otherwise conduct themselves in the future' (p. 526). The cases tend to involve shareholder consent for the transfer of assets or a takeover, and commitments by directors to make certain recommendations to shareholder or not to cooperate with rival bids.

The risk of financial consequences from a breach of the duty of care, particularly by non-executive directors, is virtually non-existent in the United States (Armour et al., 2009; Black, Cheffins & Klausner, 2006). Well-known Australian decisions demonstrate a real risk of liability for executive and non-executive directors that fail to exercise reasonable care to understand the business and implications of all decisions of the board (*ASIC* v. *Hellicar,* 286 ALR 501 (2012)). These directions push the board towards taking a more active role and towards exercising leadership over management.

The duties of directors require the directors to be each other's keepers. A number of cases have recognised that one key function of non-executive directors is to monitor the executive directors and executive management generally (see Conger & Lawler, 2009b; Roberts, McNulty & Stiles, 2005). Despite some contrary case law, the duty of care for executive directors may be higher than non-executive directors. The more recent corporate governance codes are likely to reinforce this judicial trend. Duty of good faith requires directors to report breaches by other directors. They cannot stand by and watch another director act in a breach of duty without becoming implicated.

The common law conflict of interest rule, now modified by statute, would make a decision voidable if one director had a conflict. The rule of proper purpose is different, requiring a majority of directors to be motivated by an improper purpose.

5.4 The Board and Management

Numerous good governance codes and empirical research reveal a belief that the board has a role in developing or at least inspiring corporate strategy. The relationship between the board and management is what is seen as the classic domain for the exercise of leadership – in line with the formal hierarchy of authority.

The contrary view, advanced strongly in agency cost-inspired contractarian literature, is that strategy is the province of management. The board has power to frame its relationship with management. The informational advantages of management over non-executive directors makes the delegation of authority to management credible (Aghion & Tirole, 1997).

While management may be formally accountable to the board, the freedom of management to manage may also be built to varying extent into a CEO's employment contract. The information asymmetry between the board and management, long recognised, may limit the ability of the board to develop strategy effectively. As discussed earlier, in some economic models, freedom from board meddling (outside a crisis) may be important for the senior management to perform their leadership roles within the corporation. There is clear scope for management to exercise leadership vis-à-vis the board. Board leadership requires board self-control over the potential to exercise its powers in relation to management.

The power of the board to delegate to management the day-to-day running of the company is subject to the corporate law requirements that such delegation is reasonable and monitored by the board. Something akin to the observer effect in physics seems to exist in corporate law: one cannot measure certain systems without affecting the system. The mere monitoring of management will affect management decisions, and different monitoring systems will have different effects.

Legal duties on directors make a purely passive approach to directorship untenable. This would seem to narrow the gap between legal requirements of directors and the recent governance literature ideal of boards developing and inspiring corporate strategy. At the very least, directors cannot monitor corporate strategy without affecting the content of that strategy.

Agency theory has supported a sharp distinction between governance and management: directors govern, managers manage. As noted earlier, leadership has little role to play in a model based around rational utility maximisers inhabiting the agency model. To be sure, management responds to the financial and other incentives created by the board in remuneration packages. The extent to which management respond and the alignment between the interests of the shareholders and the incentives set by management has been contested in recent years. These uncertainties and partial alignments suggest a possible role for board leadership in relation to management.

The monitoring role of directors is important, but it cannot be understood simply as a mechanism to control self-interested or objectively incompetent behaviour. The overconfidence of management critiqued in the behavioural economics literature is the charismatic leadership described in the leadership literature. The board needs to work with the CEO to encourage entrepreneurship and appropriate risk taking. The board needs to show leadership by restraining excessive risk taking by management. This should feed into the assessment of the duty of care of directors.

5.5 The Board and Stakeholders

Corporate stakeholders have different interests and will seek to advance those interests through bargaining. Key financial backers to companies frequently retain the contractual right to withdraw finance in specified circumstances. The threat to withdraw finance is likely to compel the management and/or board to enter into negotiations with the financiers. Community and environmental groups will engage not only with the broader public about corporate activities, but also the management, board and shareholders.

The role of the board is not simply a restraint on management in these circumstances. While the board may be formally obliged to act in what it believes to be the best interests of the company as a whole and as an entity, the best interests of the company cannot be identified independently of the bargaining process. A behavioural perspective (Ees, Gabrielsson & Huse, 2009) on goal formation would not assume the goals of the corporate constituents would inevitably align around the maximisation of shareholder value through maximisation of the financial capital in the fund.

If the determination of the best interests of the company is indeed a political exercise, new light is shed on the duty to act in good faith and in the best interests of the company. In discussing the board's concerns for stakeholders, the legal literature emphasises that stakeholders have claims, while firms have obligations and duties (Fassin, 2009). Without an objective function, a director's assessment of the best interests of the company will be primarily subjective. This might provide an alternative, perhaps better, explanation for the subjective nature of the duty of each director than concerns about intruding into the decision-making power of directors and the 'moral' nature of the duty. Other commentators have observed that the duty of good faith is more a duty not to act in bad faith (Summers, 1968). This usually involves the director acting for a collateral purpose or acting in circumstances where the director could reasonably be thought to have a collateral purpose. Hence the rules on conflict of interest and account of profits. Traditionalists have objected to the (occasional) judicial objectification of the duty. These cases have typically involved a failure of a director to consider a decision independently or the failure of a director (or the whole board) to consider the interests of a member of a corporate group. These 'slips' are perhaps best not seen as 'slips' into objectification, but a concern to ensure that the director is actually considering all relevant interests and balancing them. The directors acting collectively need to assess and balance all relevant interests – a political task.

The managerial interpretation centres its arguments around the board's responsibility for the company's long-term strategies. The board, as a corporate leader and core decision-making body, engages in the development of a corporate future in relation to its stakeholders (Hung, 2011). Management theorists argue that the genuine value of the board (especially non-executive directors) is their boundary-spanning contribution (see Barratt & Korac-Kakabadse, 2002; Filatotchev & Nakajima, 2014; Geletkanycz & Hambrick, 1997; Pugliese et al., 2009, among others). A director's ability to reach and involve a variety of stakeholders can be a source of competitive advantage for the company. In cases where the board determines that direct engagement with certain stakeholder groups or on specific issues is warranted, the majority takes place at the executive/operational level. The board, with its overview of the totality of the engagement, may opt for alternative or additional ways to engage with the stakeholders concerned. Stakeholder engagement can inform board decisions about the products and services that the company develops and offers, its strategic direction, its relationship with its workforce and, more broadly, the contributions and risks it poses in relation to the economic, social and natural environment (Freeman, Harrison & Zyglidopoulos, 2018). Thus, from both perspectives, directors and company officers should consider the interests of all corporate constituencies. The question, from a legal angle, is about their fiduciary duty (responsibility).

In the last decade or so, directors' responsibilities towards the company's stakeholders have been a subject of major legal debate in the Western world (see Clarke, 2014; Plessis, 2016). The most recent 'adjustments' in the sphere of corporate law have demonstrated that 'no company law system insists on boards focusing only on returns to shareholders' (Sjåfjell, 2016, p. 383). For example, the UK Companies Act 2006 (section 172.1) adopted a model that Clarke (2014) labelled a 'discretionary pluralism model' (p. 276). This model, which retains the shareholder primacy perspective, provides an inclusive list of directors' duties in relation to the interests of other stakeholders (Esser & du Plessis, 2007). In Australia, corporate law reform last took place in 2001, but the present perceptions of directors' broader accountabilities and the changing role of corporations in society point to a clear legal recognition of stakeholder interests in practice (Plessis, 2017). Canadians adopted a 'stakeholder remedy model' (Plessis, 2017, p. 41), whereby stakeholder groups can, under the Canadian Corporations Act 1995, protect or secure their interests in legal proceedings (statutory derivative actions). It seems that these changes are promoting boards' positive recognition of a broader spectrum of stakeholders. In recent legal corporate governance literature that discusses these models (Gunasekara, 2013; Plessis, 2016, 2017; Sjåfjell, 2016; Vasudev, 2013), it appears that more commonalities with the stakeholder principle in management theory are being found.

Furthermore, researchers from both camps have acknowledged major new developments in organisational forms and business cooperation in which stakeholders are becoming directly included in value creation. Many companies adopt open business models in which customers become involved in co-creation processes (Kortmann & Piller, 2016; Prahalad & Ramaswamy, 2000). Importantly, for our research, new business models promote a redefinition of the firm and its key actors, as they allow internal and external stakeholders not only to share financial profits, but also to participate in strategic decisions.

In summary, the increasing importance, power and actions of various stakeholders, their contribution to the company goals and the company's responsibility to stakeholders' well-being are documented in legal and managerial theory contributions on the subject. From numerous legal cases, it is evident that law cannot ignore these trends (see Letza, Sun & Kirkbride, 2004; Plessis, 2017; Vasudev, 2013). As Harrison and Wicks (2013) stressed, 'the total value created by a firm is the sum of the utility created for each of a firm's legitimate stakeholders' (p. 102). We agree that there are differences between claims and interests (Vasudev, 2012), legal prioritisation of company constituencies and strategic satisficing of stakeholder needs, but the primary duty of directors is intended to not just protect but also mandate a leadership role for the board in dealing with various corporate stakeholders.

5.6 Summary and Conclusion

Board leadership takes what is essentially a static view of the regard for the interests of certain stakeholders (compliance) and transforms it into one that can encompass a competitive advantage in a dynamic context. In this way, the core work of the board of directors involves building strategic relationships with those groups (stakeholders) directly or indirectly affected by a company's activities as well as those which may have a positive or negative effect on the company's ability to operate. The board is at the nexus of these relationships with its internal and external stakeholders – shareholders, management and non-shareholding stakeholders. We maintain that the board's leadership role in this nexus of relationships is better understood by an integration of key concepts and findings between the disciplines of management and law. In so doing, we contend a more comprehensive understanding of the board as the nexus of these relationships can be developed.

We reject the notion that the models based on agency costs and property rights provide an adequate and complete basis for the theory and practice of corporate governance. While advocating a more people-centred and less property-centred view of the corporation, the baby should not be thrown out with the bathwater. The agency costs and property rights model contains important insights. Our advocacy of the need to give greater consideration to people associated with a corporation and their relations with each other is consistent with recent scholarship that argues that greater importance needs to be attached to behavioural aspects of board functioning. However, corporate governance also contains rules that determine roles of shareholders, directors and, to a lesser extent, other stakeholders. The complex relationships between the board and corporate stakeholders cannot be understood in terms of principal–agent relationships and residual rights of control.

Corporate practice of modern organisations and their boards, as elaborated in numerous studies over the last two decades (for an overview, see for example, Huse, 2007, 2018; Letza, Sun & Kirkbride, 2004; Lorsch, 2017, Westphal & Zajac, 2013), confirms our points about the board as a nexus of corporate relationships. Our own research presented in the next section provides evidence of board leadership (or lack of it) for realising enormous benefit and grievous harm.

6 How Boards Exercise Leadership

This section examines board leadership enacted through four types of relationships in which competing and complementary interests are aligned/reconciled, resisted or transformed to affect board effectiveness and impact firm performance. The board, as the nexus of relationships, is expected to enact leadership among shareholders, management, directors and stakeholders for value creation and protection. We examined board leadership in a company's transition to a new ownership structure through an initial public offering in publicly held corporations and a founder-CEO-listed company. Next, we studied how positive board dynamics (or board leadership enacted among directors) contributed to the development of sound corporate strategy and ameliorated governance processes. We also explored board leadership in relation to CEO succession planning and development of a transformational chair–CEO relationship in the context of a listed (partially privatised) state-owned enterprise and a publicly listed company. Finally, we observed board leadership in building relationships with internal and external stakeholders.

Our examples, vignettes and illustrations of various types of leadership exercised by boards are generated from our in-depth case study research on leadership in governance within companies from different industries and with different ownership structures. We adopt the narrative analysis approach, arguably one of the qualitative approaches best suited to capturing the dynamic sequences of events and the temporal ordering of ideas and processes (Creswell & Poth, 2017; Langley, 1999; Vaara, Sonenshein & Boje, 2016). We track board leadership across multiple relationships, over time and events, thereby avoiding the issue of inductively leaping from a single instance to the board as a whole (Miles & Huberman, 1994). Our cases are drawn from an Anglo-Australasian context. This context, with its institutions of corporate governance, interpretations of the purpose and roles of boards of directors, as well as governance practices, influences board leadership. We are aware that the nature of relationships between corporate constituencies in different systems of corporate governance has a reflection on various aspects of board functioning and leadership (for a comparative overview of board roles, functions and designs in different systems of corporate governance, see Clarke, 2017). However, we believe that our examples provide insights into universal complexities and practicalities of board leadership.

6.1 Board Leadership in Dealing with Shareholders

6.1.1 Non-market Shareowners in the Initial Public Offering

We studied the board's role in two cases (both in the energy sector) of an initial public offering. We first present an example of the board of a state-owned enterprise, which made several proactive (but unsuccessful) attempts to transform the company's relationship with the non-market shareholder (government). The case illustrates that board leadership in setting strategic direction is tempered by government control, and efforts to reconcile conflicting visions are difficult, resulting in a forced or compromised decision. In 2011, primarily as a result of ideological commitments by the recently elected government, the board chair was advised to prepare the coal-based energy company for partial privatisation. The board had developed a dynamic, evolving relationship with the shareholder and had anticipated the potential change in the company's ownership structure. The chair approached the government with a proposal to improve the long-term risk and reward profile of the company through an energy diversification strategy that included alternative renewable energy in return for an exemption from public floatation. The board chair persisted in his efforts to engage in constructive dialogue with the government about the vision of the company, the commitment to diversify its assets base, and the role of the board in the value creation and protection for current and prospective shareholders. The government rejected all board efforts. The board learned that the government's commitment to the privatisation of all energy-based state-owned enterprises was critical for perceived economic progress and political objectives.

By 2012, the government had lost confidence that the board would implement the changes necessary for the impending initial public offering. The board realised that differences in the vision of the company and the role of the board in governing the company were insurmountable. In this context, a rapprochement between the board and shareholder (government) could not be developed in the absence of mutual commitment to develop an understanding of the differences and generate a shared strategic perspective of the future of the company. The board chair recognised that his capacity to affect the strategic direction of the company was severely constrained; he resigned. The government withdrew the company from the initial public offering process and appointed new directors, chair and management. The subsequent volatility in the coal market precluded any further privatisation initiatives.

Another energy company's initial public offering is a notable example of board leadership transforming the listing company's relationship with its non-market shareholder. The board chair of this company was skilled at using the knowledge base of directors in ways that fostered the timely and frequent sharing of knowledge among directors and with its shareholder (government). The board believed that, consistent with its role in value generation and protection, a change in ownership structure through an initial public offering was in the best interest for the future of the company. The company would be entering an already-crowded energy market as the third company making the transition from a state-owned enterprise to a mixed-ownership model in 2014. Among its initial decisions in preparing for the initial public offering, the board decided to be the first company in the country to use a new prospectus format rather than the conventional model preferred by the government. The board's decision reflected its commitment that new beliefs and practices needed to become visibly, explicitly institutionalised throughout the company. The board had weighed the choices, recognising that its twin goals of maximising share sales and minimising the risks associated with the initial public offering could be aligned with the interests of the government. A systematic process of board decisions using the mutually shared goal throughout the initial public offering aided in an integrated, coherent set of decisions and actions, including the use of the new prospectus format, for the change in ownership structure. As demonstrated through the initial public offering process, the board's leadership in identifying, interpreting and adapting to the challenges in shifting from a single shareholder to a multitude of shareholders aided in constructively shaping a dynamic new relationship with government.

6.1.2 Bloc Shareholders

The case of a large international airport company illustrates that a board can ill-afford to marginalise the interests of bloc shareholders in the pursuit of delivering strong and consistent returns for shareholders. The company was listed in 1998 when the government pursued the privatisation of infrastructural assets. Its most recent top-ten position on a domestic stock exchange was characterised by periods of both flat and strong profit growth.

In 2006, an external independent board chair was appointed as successor, following the retirement of the long-serving incumbent chair. The board decided that the company needed an infusion of capital to bring about the long-term development of its infrastructure and assets to support its new vision as the country's gateway airport. The board decided that the sale of the company to a foreign buyer would overcome the financial impediment and the new company would be well positioned to deliver strong and consistent returns for its shareholders. The board failed to inspire bloc shareholders and instil confidence that the strategy was in the interests of all shareholders. The perceived lack of engagement by the board with the bloc shareholders in the formation of the strategy resulted in shareholders' loss of confidence in the board. The board's decisions culminated in the resignation of the board chair after one year in the role, the appointment of shareholder nominee directors to the board and the re-classification of the airport as a strategic asset by the government, terminating any future foreign acquisition attempts.

6.1.3 Controlling Shareholder

In our research, we came across two listed companies with controlling shareholders. The case of a large and old retail group illustrates board dealings with an individual controlling shareholder. The company is 156 years old and is partially listed on a domestic share market. In 1988, a foreign entrepreneur acquired the company at a time when its image as an industrial retailer, coupled with high costs and low sales, had jeopardised its survival. The entrepreneur transformed the company by reconfiguring its business model, customers and stores. In 2001, the company was listed on a domestic stock exchange with the entrepreneur as the controlling shareholder acting as the managing director. The managing director drew on his own network and the network of his trusted advisors to identify board members with the distinct knowledge, skills and experiences. In developing the corporate strategy, the board sought to balance decisions for growth in sales and profits to satisfy shareholder expectations with decisions to avoid value destruction. The board did make strategic errors despite the alignment of non-independent shareholders' and managements' interests. The board decided to diversify into a new luxury retail segment. The retail group's competitive advantage derived, in part, from its ability to transfer knowledge across its two distinct brands. The company, however, lacked the capabilities to convert its low-cost retailing expertise to benefit the new high-end initiative. The board decided to exit from the luxury segment and wound down the stores.

In 2008, the retail group board recognised that embarking on a digitalisation business-to-customer strategy, led by the board, would demand understanding the nature and magnitude of the transformation to all aspects of the company, including its business model. The board had chosen to delay its entry into e-commerce, preferring an incremental, sequenced approach to enable the company to apply the insights gained from its initial internal digital initiatives applied to inventory control and product range to its subsequent digital initiatives. The continuity in board composition, including the chair, had generated a respectful candour among the directors and with management in expressing their viewpoints and having those viewpoints heard. In so doing, the directors identified a gap in their collective knowledge base of the requisite differentiated knowledge and skills required for their pursuit of the digitalisation strategy. The board closed this gap, in part, through the new appointment of a director experienced in digital retail transformation. In 2011, the board made its move to take on the e-commerce challenge more directly and launched its Web commerce strategy as the digital growth vehicle for the company. The board evolved the strategy to align the physical stores with its online presence to provide its customers with a consistent retail experience. In 2016, the board achieved its fifth consecutive year of record-setting profit with its online sales continuing to grow faster than its brick-and-mortar stores.

Our second case, a finance company, distinguished itself from the nearly 100 finance companies operating nationwide by listing on the domestic stock exchange in 2002. This finance company went from raising US$11 million on its initial prospectus to attracting new capital of US$170 million at the height of its loan offer, primarily to property developers, in 2007. The company's competitive advantage resided, in part, with its high-profile board of independent non-executive directors, which included two justice ministers and a former press officer to Her Majesty Elizabeth the Second. Due to the directors' celebrity status and long-term public service, this board was ranked as one of the most trustworthy nationally. The chair parlayed his visibility as a distinguished treaty negotiator through his testimonials in marketing materials to attract new capital from individual investors. The founder and controlling shareholder (owning approximately 65 per cent of the shares) was the company's CEO and managing director. In 2007, the board, seemingly ill-informed about the precarious financial state, approved a new prospectus and continued to promote the company to prospective investors. The board did not appear to organise its activities in order to facilitate the timely sharing of information between the directors and controlling shareholder/CEO to make better and faster decisions for long-term growth, not just current earnings. The directors did not appear to ask questions about the risks to the viability of the company given the impairment of loan repayments, challenge the accuracy of the financial statements considering significant discrepancies or discuss an audit report that detailed the magnitude of the issues. The past success of the board appeared to inculcate a sense of infallibility in the directors' decisions coupled with a lack of interest in the company's performance. The directors believed that they had made the right decisions in their role to protect shareholders' interests and increase their wealth. In 2008, the board's perfunctory approach to governance resulted in calamity. The company, unable to make payments, entered receivership, owing US$77 million to 4,400 investors. The directors were found guilty of breaching directors' duties.

6.2 Building Board Collective Capabilities

6.2.1 Creating and Mobilising Knowledge

Board leadership involves the accumulation and mobilisation of knowledge to foster new ideas, encourage constructive dissent and promote innovation. One approach to cultivating capacity to acquire and use new knowledge among directors is to further develop directors' knowledge, skills and experience through personal professional learning development so that their participation in wealth creation activities adds value. In this way, board leadership involves a recognition of the cognitive diversity within a board as a strength and is accompanied by processes to enable the board to reconcile diverse perspectives.

This aspect of board leadership is illustrated well by a large bank operating for almost 160 years. The bank faced fundamental shifts in the industry, increased competition and threats to its positioning. The board, an early adopter of gender diversity in the selection and appointment of directors, supported the creation of an ad hoc committee to recommend ways to improve the bank's profitability through a strategy of diversity and inclusion. The committee, supported by a consultant, prepared and delivered fact-based material and professional development activities to improve the directors' and management's ability to understand diversity and transform it into a competitive advantage. In a range of diversity workshops, the exploration of directors' personal perspectives fostered open debate, created space for the emergence of new ideas and enabled an integration of perspectives, which compelled support for the company-wide implementation of the strategy. The diversity strategy, supported by policy and practice, flowed throughout the company, achieving the reconfiguration of conventional operating processes from employee selection and recruitment to the creation of new specialised client business units.

The board also enacted a complementary approach to facilitating knowledge building at the individual director level by assembling a diverse knowledge base at the board level. The board specified diversity in the selection criteria for the appointment of new directors to increase knowledge of cultures and markets as a competitive imperative. Board appointment decisions that placed a high value on factors such as age, gender, education and language aided in the acceleration of the board's capacity to cultivate an understanding of diverse markets.

6.2.2 Board Leadership to Institutionalise Governance Processes

In the case of a software development company, poor governance practices, which had resulted in multiple violations of the domestic stock exchange listing rules, illustrate how leadership enacted by the board chair and newly appointed independent directors brought about the transformation of the board's governance practices. Following his 24 per cent ownership stake in the company, the board chair challenged the persistent governance failures and envisioned a board that added value to the young company's growth and profitability. The transformation unfolded in two phases: a clear assessment of the board's structure and processes and directors' capabilities, and engagement with the directors and CEO to develop and integrate new practices. Each phase entailed leadership enacted individually and collectively by the chair and the directors: the first involved generating director support for the assessment, and the second, implementing new governance practices.

The new independent directors, empowered by the chair, conducted a detailed assessment with the assistance of two law firms given the company's incorporation in the United States and its listing on a foreign stock exchange. The review and analysis encompassed the initial public offering from five years earlier to contemporary board practices, exposing the depth and magnitude of the board's oversights and listing violations. The chair accepted the report and, through the collective efforts of all directors, the board was able to come to terms with the vulnerabilities for the company created by the persistent lack of governance processes. A shared understanding emerged among the directors which confirmed that the identified risks required visible and comprehensive action that combined immediate implementation along with a long-term orientation to generate transformational change.

Desired behaviours and practices in the board's change process were brought about by the leadership enacted by the chair, the directors and new senior management. A sustained collective commitment among the directors to ensure the company's market leadership position as the world's most widely used board portal service served as a powerful mechanism to cultivate effective governance processes and practices and resolve threats to the company's reputation, profitability and viability as a listed company.

6.3 Developing Board–Management Relationships

6.3.1 Board Leadership in CEO Succession Planning

The case of an airline, a national flag carrier, represents a remarkable example of board leadership in the dynamic design and implementation of a CEO succession process for long-term value creation. The airline was the first mixed-ownership company listed on the domestic stock exchange, with the government as its largest shareowner. The board had discretion in its consideration of each CEO's appointment in the company's evolution. The board's success in identifying and attracting international CEO talent over fifteen years resulting in three CEO appointments can be traced to board leadership in synthesising diverse knowledge bases to inform a coherent strategy and a set of decisions and actions. The board facilitated an open and rich dialogue about envisioning the future of the company which allowed for an evolving strategic direction for the company. It also informed the collective board decision of the desired knowledge, skills and capabilities in a prospective CEO to bring about the emerging strategy. The board explored widely each time to identify candidates internal and external to the company as well as within and outside of the industry, which gave them the advantage of attracting and selecting candidates that would help the company in its goal to capture and sustain market leadership. Board leadership in developing a planned, repeatable and regular process for CEO succession created, in part, the company's competitive advantage.

6.3.2 Cultivating Board Chair–CEO Leadership

Leadership is enacted by board chairs and CEOs as they build and evolve a relationship over time. They engage in processes to cultivate an adaptable relationship in the face of changing conditions. Consider another illustration of a different chair–CEO relationship of the previously mentioned international airport, which reflected an evolution and adaptation of the CEO's experience. Initially, the chair drew from her own experience as a CEO to cultivate a mentor relationship with the first-time CEO of the airport. The chair guided the transition of the former executive manager to his new role as a CEO, providing feedback, support and resources. Following her retirement from the board, a new chair and CEO developed a tight–loose relationship that created a space to ask questions, foster innovation and encourage exploration in crafting solutions to organisational issues. The mutual experience acquired by the CEO and chair through their interactions over time reflected the dynamic nature of their coaching relationship.

Leadership enacted between the CEO and board involves flexibility to respond to challenges and seize opportunities that may create long-lasting value for the company. The transition from a start-up (entrepreneurial) company to a listed company presents an opportunity for founder-CEOs to formalise informal systems and routinise improvisational processes to aid in value creation. As noted earlier, the board has a role in serving as a source of value creation. In engaging with founder-CEOs, the board acts to ensure accountability by guiding and shaping decisions and instilling integrity in the behaviours of management and the veracity of financial data. Boards help to create value through the development and refinement of a viable long-term strategy by focusing founder-CEOs efforts on gaining access to different resources, building new skills and capabilities, and identifying opportunities for growth. The case of a software company illustrates how the relationship between a founder-CEO and a compliant board led to a calamitous outcome – the resignation and conviction of the founder-CEO. That was the first case of market manipulation in New Zealand. The founder-CEO had become the 'face' (brand) of the technology company, featuring prominently in the marketing materials. He developed an international blue-chip client base, persuasively articulating a compelling vision for the company to become the global leader in how board materials are produced, delivered and reviewed. In 2007, as the founder-CEO prepared the company for an initial public offering on the domestic stock market, five experienced international and domestic independent directors and a chair were appointed to the board to complement the four executive directors. The initial public offering did not unfold as the board anticipated. An ethical lapse by the board and founder in their failure to reveal his role as a director of a bankrupt company impaired the company's share sales. The founder resigned within twenty-four hours of the initial public offering from his CEO role but retained his role as a director. The board concluded that the founder was instrumental to value creation as he had the knowledge, skills and experience to lead growth opportunities.

One year later, the board restructured; the chair and international directors resigned. The board struggled to operationalise governance systems and processes to protect and generate shareholder wealth. Efforts were complicated, in part, by asymmetric knowledge among the directors of domestic listing rules and a US-incorporated company. Board leadership for identifying and bridging this gap through creating knowledge-sharing opportunities did not emerge. The directors remained focused on growth opportunities. They did not appear to recognise that the risk incurred by their failure to ask questions would have long-term unintended consequences. Unknown to the board, the former CEO had access to the domestic stock exchange trading system. He engaged in stock manipulation by artificially changing the share prices without any change in ownership of the shares. The former CEO, who retained a 20 per cent ownership in the company, claimed his actions resulted in minimal negative impact for shareholders. His explanations positioned him simultaneously as a 'victim' of bad advice from the board in not disclosing his full background and as an inept trader for failing to grasp the concept of illegal trading. He remained impervious to the deleterious effect of his actions for the company he founded.

6.4 Board Engagement with Stakeholders

In the context of complex and dynamic relationships among different corporate constituencies, boards are expected to play a stronger role in dealing with non-shareholder and non-management stakeholders. The process of developing board–stakeholder engagements is multidimensional. A company and its sta-keholders can be involved in different power relations and stakeholders can proactively or reactively (stakeholder- or board-initiated actions) participate in the company's governance processes. Stakeholder engagement can range from stakeholder dialogue, such as multi-stakeholder forums, to strategic collabora-tions. We illustrate different forms of board–stakeholder relationships with examples from two companies.

6.4.1 Board Proactive Approach in Encouraging Stakeholder Dialogue

The first case describes the board's role in re-establishing the relationship with a company's indigenous community. The chair of an energy company, at the very beginning of her tenure, decided to resolve a twelve-year-long court case with a local community (although she was told that was not her 'job' and the company lawyers were confident of winning the case). In her actions and dealings with the management and board of the company, the chair was led by her beliefs that the company needed to (re-)establish good relationships with the community (and winning in court would not win the support of the community). She directly approached the community leader and the whole board and CEO attended various informal gatherings and formal meetings until the final resolution was sought. Although having a formal responsibility to promote shareholder interests, the board decided to meet the interests of the indigenous stakeholder even if such a decision resulted in marginally reduced profitability for several years. The resolution of the problem with this stake-holder, however, allowed the company to be commercially effective in the long run.

The chair proved to be a critical relationship builder, shaping the process of engagement and coordination that enabled the effective resolution of the problem, and implementing ideas that benefitted both the stakeholder and the company. Throughout the following years, the board continued to engage in a broad and regular dialogue with this stakeholder, which resulted in further commercial gains for the company and social benefits for the community.

6.4.2 Crisis Management through Stakeholder Participation on the Board

The second example portrays the appointment of a prominent union leader to the board of directors of an airline, a national flag carrier, in 2002. This appointment was unprecedented in the country's corporate governance practice. After a major financial and operational crisis in 2001, the airline had to undertake major workforce restructuring, primarily in the engineering division. Having around 11,000 employees at the time, and a long history of industrial issues, the chair of the board initiated this appointment. Most directors supported the nomination of this director, trusting that such an addition to the board would benefit the governance and whole company during this difficult period. In this situation, the directors believed that they had a responsibility towards employee stakeholders but did not have expertise and experience to understand and deal with the issue. The board needed someone with a reputation and legitimacy that would be able to have an effective dialogue with the employees and their representatives, while also understanding the position of the board and management.

This was a situation in which the engineering workforce and its union could damage the company's international competitive position and reputation. Hence, the board decided to engage with this stakeholder at the participatory level. In other words, the union leader as a representative of the employee stakeholder was invited to participate in the board's decision-making processes and co-create specific corporate policies. This engagement, however, was of a limited time frame. The union leader resigned from the board after his first mandate during which the organisational restructuring issues were settled.

7 Leadership in Governance

The idea that corporate boards need to demonstrate leadership is becoming a popular highlight in the business press and portals (see, for example, Deloitte Development LLC, 2016; Gibby, 2016; Lorsch & Clark, 2008), a trending research topic in the scholarly literature (e.g., Useem, Carey & Charan, 2016; Vandewaerde et al., 2011; Yar Hamidi & Gabrielsson, 2014a) and one of the principal references in various policy documents (see, for example, the UK Corporate Governance Code 2018 published by the Financial Reporting Council (2018) and a paper on board renewal in Canada published by the Canadian Institute of Corporate Directors (2015)). In practice, we know that some boards are better able to adapt and lead, and that effective leadership processes developed over time impact on a host of organisational outcomes.

In the scholarly literature, leadership of and on the board has been usually a part of the discussion on board effectiveness. Several studies have proposed that the actual behavioural dynamics of the board influences its leadership capacity and effectiveness (Gabrielsson, Huse & Minichilli, 2007; Huse & Gabrielsson, 2012; Useem, Carey & Charan, 2016). Other researchers have untangled the processes and factors pertaining to board effectiveness and leadership (e.g., Ees, Gabrielsson & Huse, 2009; Vandewaerde et al., 2011). Some scholars have suggested that the role of the board chair can potentially be understood in terms of the leadership required to fulfil different responsibilities (e.g., Harrison & Murray, 2012; Leblanc, 2005; Levrau & van den Berghe, 2013; Yar Hamidi & Gabrielsson, 2014b).

While these studies make some progress towards a more refined view of board effectiveness, theories of leadership and governance have been developing mostly separately and warrant further integration. In this Element, we contribute to this integration by introducing the leadership-in-governance view. In our conceptual discussion (Section 5) and empirical illustrations (Section 6), we elaborated on three important intersections at which governance and leadership processes can come together in any organisation: leadership of the board in relation to external stakeholders, team leadership on the board including the chair's leadership, and strategic leadership by the board in relation to management. In what follows, we review the recent developments in board leadership research and highlight the role of board leadership in strategy making.

7.1 Developments in Board Leadership Research

Traditionally, corporate board research has tended to emphasise a static, one-dimensional view of board roles, tasks and composition that narrowly emphasises the central importance of developing a normative approach to research rather than a more expansive, dynamic and thickly descriptive approach to the subject. Researchers, however, have discovered new ways of conceptualising the work of the board by breaking away from the theoretical frameworks that have historically dominated the field and have applied new approaches in an effort to generate some fresh understanding of the complexities inherent to the work of boards. Some authors have embraced a paradoxical approach and focused on the importance of the dynamic balance between control and collaboration (Sundaramurthy & Lewis, 2003) and independence and interdependence (Huse, 1994) in board processes. Others have applied the life cycle approach and emphasised the importance of evolutionary theory in understanding the dynamics of board roles and tasks (e.g., Filatotchev, Toms & Wright, 2006; Lynall, Golden & Hillman, 2003; Perrault & McHugh, 2015). Yet another significant conceptual movement brings to the fore the investigation of actual rather than supposed board behaviour. This involves viewing the board through a behavioural perspective lens (Ees, Gabrielsson & Huse, 2009; Huse, 2005, 2007; Westphal & Zajac, 2013).

The fundamental principles of behavioural theory assume that the purpose of the board is to add value to the corporation by aiding it, not in the sense of maintaining control over it, but through communication and collaboration, 'engaging in collective processes of search and discovery' (Ees, Gabrielsson & Huse, 2009, p. 308). Legislation may serve a purpose in realigning the intentions of directors and executives 'straying from the path of good governance' (Kocourek, Burger & Birchard, 2003, p. 6), but good governance in the real sense will only occur when the individuals concerned consciously choose to govern well. In the situation where governance is reduced to a checklist exercise, the potential for leadership is lost; there is no space for leadership to express itself through discernment, discussion and good decision-making. It is through the lens of behavioural theory that researchers can begin to explore notions of leadership and leadership processes in board development.

We suggest that the primary purpose of the board is to provide leadership, although this has not yet been properly ingrained in common understandings or theoretical conceptualisations of governance literature. Some progress has been made by several scholars in bringing leadership and governance perspectives together, but this effort has been isolated and predominantly conceptual (e.g., Davies, 2006; Holloway & van Rhyn, 2005; Machold et al., 2011; Pye, 2002).

The essence of the leadership-in-governance view is to move beyond the boundaries of 'performance and conformance functions' of the board (Tricker, 1994) and to look towards the future (Casal & Caspar, 2014). The transition of board members from organisational controllers and monitors to organisational leaders has been welcomed as a positive development by many corporate governance commentators (Financial Reporting Council, 2018; Gibby, 2016). Organisational stakeholders expect their governors to represent and respond, not just dictate results and define problems or command solutions. These expectations, which closely resemble leadership virtues, demonstrate a radical movement from orthodox components of governance (e.g., finance, strategy, facilities) to deeper and potentially more powerful facets of governance (e.g., values, beliefs, mission, agendas) (Chait, Ryan & Taylor, 2005). 'Discovering' governance as a leadership activity, that is, seeing governance as a multidimensional practice can enhance stakeholders' trust and commitment to the organisation. Moreover, it can serve to improve the effectiveness of boards (Huse, 2007).

There are two extant streams of research into the context of board leadership (Huse, Gabrielsson & Minichilli, 2009). The first looks at the boardroom dynamics or actual board behaviour (e.g., Bezemer, Nicholson & Pugliese, 2018; Huse & Zattoni, 2008; Nicholson, Pugliese & Bezemer, 2017). Developing trust between the board members and having open and honest interactions within the board and with the CEO are considered important preconditions for effective governance. Although directors are elected or appointed to the board because of their individual skills and knowledge, they work as a group (Huse, 2007). In a group, people work with each other, and the final outcome is the result of their joint efforts. Therefore, they are dependent on each other. Through their relationships, directors develop a specific boardroom culture (Leblanc & Gillies, 2005) which, to provide for an effective board's functioning, needs to balance trust and distrust (Nooteboom, 1996), and closeness and distance, as well as consensus and conflict in the boardroom. Many authors (e.g., Barratt & Korac-Kakabadse, 2002; Gautier, 2002; Huse & Gabrielsson, 2012) argue that more research is required within the context of the boardroom to understand what can be changed to encourage talented individuals and executives to thrive in the board environment. Gray (2007) points out that the overemphasis placed upon structural aspects of governance has lulled shareholders into 'a false sense of security … and has led many boards to ignore the less visible, but more important cultural and procedural aspects of governance' (p. 61).

The second stream of research puts the accent on the board as a value-creating team (Huse, 2007). The concept of 'adding value' is broad and incorporates constructs such as improving board interrelationships to enable more healthy and robust discussion, and utilising board members strengths to create a well-balanced team. Adding value is closely related to the purpose of the board, to the performance function and to effective organisational leadership (Huse, 2018). Building on early team production studies (e.g., Blair & Stout, 1999; Kaufman & Englander, 2005), Gabrielsson, Huse & Minichilli (2007) and Machold et al. (2011), among others, pointed out the importance of knowledgeable members on the board and a skilled and competent team leader for value creation. According to the team production model, directors should behave as team members, both within the boardroom and in their relationship with management, and they need to have experience and resources strategically important to the organisation. By including knowledge and skills that different board members possess, a board enhances its ability to govern strategic abilities (Klarner, Yoshikawa & Hitt, 2018). Such a board would be capable of assisting the company to create and sustain competitive advantage (Huse & Gabrielsson, 2012). The gains that such a board can produce arise from cooperation. In other words, to perform as a team, members of the board need to be able to acquire, absorb and understand strategic information, to communicate the information among themselves and with the senior management team, to influence the strategic orientation of the company, and to communicate their decisions and major changes with other inside and outside stakeholders.

Our perspective differs from team production because we consider the company from the perspective of the board as leader. If we consider these activities as part of the influence process which facilitates the performance of the board, we can see that they all illuminate various aspects of leadership such as group processes, power relations, personality or competence qualities. More specifically, these activities are the components of what is described as transformational leadership. According to this approach to leadership, it is the transformation beyond the transaction (the basis of human interactions) that enables followers to perform beyond expectations (Jackson & Parry, 2018). It has been shown that transformational leadership supports team effectiveness (Jung & Sosik, 2002), individual performance (Jung & Avolio, 2000) and entrepreneurial behaviour (Engelen et al., 2015). Our research on leadership in governance, discussed and presented in this Element, demonstrates how governing boards and directors, collectively and individually, can foster transformational leadership throughout the organisation.

7.2 Board Leadership and Strategy

Once board members understand the organisational context and their purpose, the hope is that they may conceive of ways in which they can individually and collectively contribute to adding value to the organisation. The board's contribution to strategy making is an important value-adding activity and something that is genuinely considered to be the purest demonstration of the board's leadership role. Although this is widely recognised within the management literature and in conventional governance practice, the nature of and extent to which the board should be actively involved in shaping strategy is still highly controversial and hotly debated within the corporate governance literature (for comprehensive literature reviews, see Aberg et al., 2017; Pugliese et al., 2009).

For a long time, a directorship has been conceived of by many corporate governance theorists as a one-dimensional job that entails control and monitoring. While many notable high-performing companies have compellingly demonstrated the active role of boards in strategy shaping, research (e.g., Lorsch & MacIver, 1989; Machold & Farquhar, 2013; Siciliano, 2005) has shown that board members are still not utilised anywhere near as much as they could and should be. The net result of being shut out of the strategy-formulation process (in other than a token rubber-stamping way) is that many board members become disillusioned and ineffectual because they believe that they are not able to add real value to the organisation.

Researchers and practitioners argue that it is of vital importance for any organisation to have an active and engaged board. A number of studies (e.g., Carter & Lorsch, 2004; Hendry, Kiel & Nicholson, 2010; McNulty & Pettigrew, 1999; Pettigrew & McNulty, 1995; Ravasi & Zattoni, 2006; Stiles & Taylor, 2001; Zahra & Filatotchev, 2004) have revealed that increased involvement on the part of directors in strategy formulation, strategic decision-making and strategic restructuring leads to higher levels of firm performance, especially in situations of environmental uncertainty (Geletkanycz & Hambrick, 1997; Siciliano, 2005). Furthermore, numerous empirical investigations provide evidence of board involvement in various strategies, such as innovation strategy, R&D strategies, internationalisation and strategic change (for an overview of the studies, see Pugliese et al., 2009).

Taking a leadership perspective, the board can and should provide active support to management in strategy formulation and implementation (Huse, 2007). Among shareholders, there is a growing demand for directors to play an active rather than a passive role in guiding a company's future development (Ingley et al., 2011). By drawing upon their external knowledge and expertise, board members are well-positioned to advise management on strategic issues facing the company and provide them with access to external resources. Through these activities, directors support and empower management, thus contributing to the company's strategic competitive advantage. The comprehensiveness of this role is especially emphasised in smaller organisations on their transitional stages (Zahra & Filatotchev, 2004).

Yet strategic transformation is often disruptive, risky and costly. It is not surprising that directors of boards find themselves governing companies encumbered with so many different ways dedicated to reinforcing the status quo. But left unchecked, a penchant for risk avoidance can find a board governing a sluggish, relatively stagnant organisation, leaving the window open for competitors to shake up markets. In other words, over-reliance on boards'

monitoring responsibility has the tendency to stifle board leadership for stimulating a value-creating strategy. For that reason, the favoured position of shareholders as stakeholders ex ante in the appointment of directors and ex post
ensuring accountability formally through the general meeting and informally
through influence should not be viewed as problematic but instead a mechanism
to ensure boards continued focus on generating value.

Boards committed to strategic renewal, adaptation and growth may benefit from three leadership-in-governance insights: opportunity exploration,
strategic selection and mobilisation. Much like a triangle, all three enablers
come together, affecting each other's development iteratively. Although
they are simultaneously in play, at any given point in time, one of the
processes will need greater attention by the board. Moreover, each process
operates among and between directors, who themselves need to interact
with investors and stakeholders and senior management (the CEO). The
processes critically reside within how well the board successfully shapes
interactions as the situation evolves and the necessity for strategic change
intensifies.

7.2.1 Board Engagement in Opportunity Exploration

In this process – opportunity exploration – board leadership creates the
relationship among directors, with senior management and between share-
holders/stakeholders to continually pose and consider options for positioning
the company where opportunities are most promising given the context within
which they operate. Leadership action is required for board members to be in
constant engagement with ideas. These actions allow for re-envisioning and
new paths to success to emerge from anyone regardless of experience or title at
any time. The conventional approach, firmly etched in the practice of many
boards, in which the CEO devises strategy and the board provides approval or
holds out for changes, is eclipsed by these processes. It is essential for the
board to learn quickly, stay alert to industry trends and keep an eye on the
competition.

These processes also involve cultivating a receptivity to creativity and openness, encouraging exploration and fostering cooperation across perspectives.
This means that the board dynamics and the board–CEO relationship for
strategy formation shifts from an orderly, predictable and sequential (hierarchical) process to a dynamic, fluid and iterative one with a collaborative orientation. Through this process, board and management collectively create a space
for new ideas to emerge, encourage open communication and constructive
dissent, and promote lively involvement.

7.2.2 Board Role in Enabling Strategic Selections

Strategic selection is the second board leadership process for bringing about transformation. To do so, board leadership coalesces and aligns a distinct combination of value-creating opportunities that involve reallocation of resources to transform the business. The generation and acceptance of ideas for reallocation involve refocusing organisational energies to where there is a clear sense of, and commitment to, a shared desirable future state. With the articulation of a shared organisational purpose, board leadership inspires investors, stakeholders and senior management by translating new growth-opportunity concepts into reality.

Because the outcome of strategic transformation cannot be fully predicted, it follows that returns may not emerge quickly enough for short-term investors because of the long gestation required to fulfil the future mandate. Short-term investor demands for immediate profit need to be reconciled with long-term strategic growth orientation. After all, taking a (reasonably) performing company into uncertain terrain, despite the end goal clearly in mind, requires board leadership that has the confidence to be decisive, the courage to change course when necessary and the support of its stakeholders that the board's activities will enhance competitive advantage.

To deal with the short-/long-term contradictions, a board can strategically select short-term initiatives anchored in a long-term strategic framework, positioned as new opportunities to be gained for unlocking the growth potential from a company's core business. Such a strategic framework can provide enough flexibility for a board to examine, explore, challenge and ultimately choose which options to pursue and which ones to leave aside without being prescriptive. This approach can allow a board to focus its decisions on those initiatives that provide long-term growth and minimise their time and opportunity cost of less significant or ill-timed initiatives. The adoption of such a framework also accelerates decision-making as emergent opportunities become known.

7.2.3 Board Leadership in Mobilising Strategic Actions

The third board leadership process for strategic transformation is to enable mobilisation. Board leadership which enables mobilisation eschews spot checking at random or designated points in favour of continuous engagement which limits negative surprises and promotes deeper, more nuanced insights for long-term growth. A board enables this by building new relationships and maintaining existing ones with senior management, stakeholders and among directors before they falter. By expressing a sincere interest in their opinions and seeking out similarities with others, board leadership fosters a shared purpose and a supportive climate. All too often, boards take a sporadic interest in perfunctory assessments of strategic performance, sending signals to shareholders and senior management that corrective action is needed. Continuous engagement – through systematic processes of interaction – is required.

Often, among directors, the major challenge is as much about gaining an understanding of (and strengthening) the relationships that shape a company's assets and processes, as it is one of letting go of outmoded processes and policies that impede growth. It is essential that a board frequently challenges the established system and conventional approaches and also anticipates the rewards which would be satisfying in helping a company grow.

Perhaps one of the most profound challenges of board leadership involves enabling mobilisation among and between directors. A board of directors is situated at the most important intersection of different perspectives, and as such, they have to deal with the changes among and between shareholders, management and each other. They should repeatedly remind each other of what they are seeking to accomplish and what is at stake. They need to find ways to provide mutual support informed, in part, by the expertise and experience each director brings to the board discussion. They draw upon that knowledge to foster consensus and demonstrate the ability to disagree with the ideas proposed by each other without neither being disagreeable nor jeopardising the cohesiveness of the board. If a board is to work as a strategic group, then all members' actions need to be intentional, coordinated and invested in building the collective capability of the organisation. For example, the board of an international airport we observed had a very successful process of mobilising actions related to strategy shaping. Annually, the board and CEO would jointly select which facets of the business to investigate as a potential growth initiative. In this way, both the board and senior management shared responsibility for the strategic trajectory of the company over the near future and the longer term. For each of these sessions, directors and senior management were invited to suspend any predetermined solutions and engage in a discussion to explore strategic opportunities. Background papers, sent out in advance of the session by the board, added substance to these vibrant interactive sessions. The agreed-upon strategic options and plans would be reviewed regularly in subsequent board meetings.

7.3 Board Leadership Challenge: Implications for Directors

For boards seeking to make the shift from familiar decision control to encompass the full spectrum of strategic decision-making, our research unveils an iterative process that may be used for integration. Boards will need to relinquish deeply engrained practices wherein the opportunity for the identification of future revenue-generating streams is the sole responsibility of senior management (CEOs). In today's less predictable environment where opportunities are more diffuse, boards bring experience and expertise from other industries which can inform their capacity to spot opportunities to meet growing needs.

Boards will have to overcome their reliance on a collection of insightful individuals to gain the full potential of the team. Strategy needs to continuously evolve as the competitive landscape changes with technological innovation, new entrants, and different services and products. Boards, like strategy, cannot live in the past. Yesterday's successes cannot overtake today's concerns about how markets and competitors are changing. Boards of directors require an ability to foster a team approach which supports and questions proposals when they are made, inspires new ideas and direction when obstacles are encountered, exemplifies valued behaviour and adapts their individual coaching/mentoring.

Achieving ideal board dynamics requires moving from an individualised notion of leadership, such as a star director or a heroic board chair, to a collective approach involving a contested and negotiated set of relationships. The skills required to successfully negotiate this complex environment are extensive and may be too broad to be possessed by one leader (Alvarez & Svejenova, 2005; O'Toole, Galbraith & Lawler, 2002). Thus, the impact of board leadership on strategic transformation goes well beyond the motivating effect of an inspirational leader. Collaboration at the corporate level improves the success of the strategic organisational partnership (Huxham & Vangen, 2000), allowing top corporate managers and directors adequate attention for different aspects of the leadership task including operational activities and long-term strategy (Bass, 1990). Board leadership bridges the conflicting perspectives to guide decisions and actions that help to build a shared vision as well as influence organisational design and allocation of resources. The pay-off is an active and engaged board committed to its role in both successfully formulating and implementing strategy.

For organisations to thrive and evolve, board leadership is needed to instil a capacity for adaptation. It is rarely a spontaneous act. When it comes to strategic renewal, board leadership plays a critical role in both what it chooses to do and how it chooses to do it. The creation and adjustment of strategies to position a company for long-term value creation appears to be a collective endeavour, one that benefits from engagement with individual directors, management and shareholders/stakeholders. The board, positioned at the intersection of different, sometimes conflicting, perspectives, makes the best possible decision for the company to create an integrated strategic direction for long-term growth. In each process, the capacity for board leadership affects the outcome. In this way, opportunity exploration, strategic selection and mobilisation are interactive processes used by boards to bring about transformation. Changes in one affect the others dynamically, initiating changes in how they evolve over time.

8 Conclusion

Some companies have boards which show a deftness in enacting leadership-in-governance to promote viability and sustainability. Those boards astutely balance processes, build relationships and determine effective resource allocation for value creation. Others do not. Much remains to be learned about the underlying processes, mechanisms and outcomes associated with boards of directors in theory and practice. The aim of this Element has been to promote an understanding of the board as the nexus of leadership and governance by providing a synthesis and integration of related concepts in the corporate governance and leadership fields.

To achieve this objective, we have examined key theoretical debates and thorny questions in an effort to understand how these literatures link together and how they can be integrated into a more meaningful understanding of the board as the nexus of leadership and governance for academics and practitioners. A model of the modern company was introduced as an entity, that is, as a corporate legal person that is an incorporation comprised of a capital fund but which acquires and generates other forms of value or capital as it operates in the world. In this model of the corporation, the fund develops to include varieties of capital, such as tangible and intangible assets. As repositories of capital and power, companies engender responsibilities which reside with the board. The company has two decision-making bodies or organs but in its operations in the world normatively, the company is animated by the board.

The board sits at the nexus of corporate participants who interact with the company in the world, balancing, at any time, the interests of different stakeholders. We examined how a board of a modern company might exercise leadership (i.e. agency) to meet its responsibilities. We incorporated insights drawn from multiple perspectives to further develop leadership in governance enacted by boards of directors. We have highlighted three intersections in which governance and leadership processes come together at the board: team leadership on the board, the chair's leadership of the board and strategic leadership by the board. We empirically illustrated board leadership in governance, exposing dynamic negotiated relationships in the interplay between governance practices and legal rules. A key implication is that boards have a more expansive and critical role in the governance and leadership of companies than previously considered. We assert that understanding the board as the nexus of leadership and governance shows how leadership can affect corporate governance arrangements and governance can sustain corporate leadership.

A contribution of this Element has been to sketch the boundaries of each of the key field's domains and highlight linkages that may have only been considered peripherally previously. Although there are topics chiefly being studied in one field (e.g., the nature of the company in corporate governance) and topics in which one field is more advanced in its theoretical development (e.g., processes of leader-follower influence in leadership), there are multiple topics that are being studied by corporate governance and leadership researchers in parallel. Researchers are studying the same phenomenon – boards of directors – from different perspectives and methodologies. Some of the most promising opportunities for scholars from each of these fields may be to become more conversant and develop a working appreciation of the significant influences of the other and interlinkages between them.

One step towards the conceptual integration of governance and leadership is the recognition that there are multiple literature bases. Researchers have not typically put these literatures together to suggest new research insights. Researchers typically lean towards literature drawn from one field. While researchers are likely to anchor their work in one field, it is important to acknowledge (and potentially incorporate) some insights from multiple perspectives. There is a growing appreciation for multi-theoretical and multi-disciplinary research in governance and leadership. The current body of research in corporate governance includes a recognition of multi-theoretical and multidisciplinary research (e.g., Huse, 2018; Tricker, 2000; Zahra & Pearce, 1989) as well as the recognition of the limitations of a single theoretical approach (particularly agency theory) to our understanding of boards of directors specifically and governance in general. In leadership, scholars acknowledge the need for integrative perspectives that consider how disparate leadership theories relate (Anderson & Sun, 2017; Dinh et al., 2014; Jackson & Parry, 2018). The speed of development and the burgeoning of leadership theories has meant that it is hard to gain a cumulative sense of the field, identifying potential commonalities and differences for one or more problems of importance for an understanding of board leadership. Leadership researchers have begun to build the case for multi-theoretical and multidisciplinary research (Avolio, Walumbwa & Weber, 2009; Gardner et al., 2010; Jackson & Parry, 2018).

Another way to extend our knowledge may be to engage in interdisciplinary research, as scholars become familiar with key theoretical debates and methodologies in each other's research communities. We see potential in the further theoretical development of leadership in governance and invite researchers in the fields to work together in joint projects. Further empirical research on leadership in governance offers unprecedented opportunities that might contribute to our understanding of board leadership as a process where competing interests are reconciled, resisted or transformed in a dynamic tension affecting board effectiveness and influencing firm performance.

To conclude, we hope this provides researchers in corporate governance and leadership with a wide lens of how these fields relate to one another, complementing and expanding an understanding of the board as the nexus for enacting leadership in governance. There is much to be learned from the experience and developments of the other. It is a different way of generating knowledge but is one that holds out promise to both academics and practitioners.

References

Aberg, C., Bankewitz, M., Knockaert, M., & Huse, M. (2017). The service tasks of board of directors: A critical literature review and research agenda. *Academy of Management Annual Meeting Proceedings*, **2017**(1).

Adams, R. B., Hermalin, B. E., & Weisbach, M. S. (2010). The role of boards of directors in corporate governance: A conceptual framework and survey. *Journal of Economic Literature*, **48**(1), 58–107.

Aghion, P., & Tirole, J. (1997). Formal and real authority in organizations. *Journal of Political Economy*, **105**(1), 1–29.

Aguilar, L. A. (2015, October 14). The Important Work of Boards of Directors. Retrieved 12 December 2018, from www.sec.gov/news/speech/important-work-of-boards-of-directors.html.

Alvarez, J. L., & Svejenova, S. (2005). *Sharing Executive Power: Roles and Relationships at the Top*. Cambridge: Cambridge University Press.

Anderson, M. H., & Sun, P. Y. (2017). Reviewing leadership styles: Overlaps and the need for a new 'full-range' theory. *International Journal of Management Reviews*, **19**(1), 76–96.

Armour, J., Black, B., Cheffins, B., & Nolan, R. (2009). Private enforcement of corporate law: An empirical comparison of the United Kingdom and the United States. *Journal of Empirical Legal Studies*, **6**(4), 687–722.

ASIC V. Hellicar, 286 ALR (2012).

Attenborough, D. (2006). The Company Law Reform Bill: An analysis of directors' duties and the objective of the company. *The Company Lawyer*, **27**(6), 162–9.

Avolio, B. J., Walumbwa, F. O., & Weber, T. J. (2009). Leadership: Current theories, research, and future directions. *Annual Review of Psychology*, **60**, 421–49. https://doi.org/10.1146/annurev.psych.60.110707.163621.

Bainbridge, S. M. (2003). Director Primacy: The means and ends of corporate governance. *Northwestern University Law Review*, **97**(2), 547–606.

Baker, S. (2016, July 12). Theresa May's Plan to Put Workers on Boards Is Borrowed from Germany and France. Retrieved 11 December 2018, from www.independent.co.uk/news/business/news/theresa-may-board-corporate-plan-germany-france-productivity-economics-a7132221.html.

Barratt, R., & Korac-Kakabadse, N. (2002). Developing reflexive corporate leadership: The role of the non executive director. *Corporate Governance: The International Journal of Business in Society*, **2**(3), 32–36.

Bass, B. M. (1990). From transactional to transformational leadership: Learning to share the vision. *Organizational Dynamics*, **18**(3), 751–60.

Bass, B. M., Avolio, B. J., Jung, D. I., & Berson, Y. (2003). Predicting unit performance by assessing transformational and transactional leadership. *Journal of Applied Psychology*, **88**(2), 207–18.

Bass, B. M., & Riggio, R. E. (2006). *Transformational Leadership*, 2nd edn. Mahwah, NJ: Lawrence Erlbaum Associates.

Bass, B. M., & Steidlmeier, P. (1999). Ethics, character, and authentic transformational leadership behavior. *The Leadership Quarterly*, **10**(2), 181–217.

Bebchuk, L. A. (2013). The myth that insulating boards serves long-term value. *Columbia Law Review*, **113**, 1637–94.

Berle, A. A. (1931). Corporate powers as powers in trust. *Harvard Law Review*, **44**(7), 1049–74.

Berle, A. A. (1965). The impact of the corporation on classical economic theory. *The Quarterly Journal of Economics*, **79**(1), 25–40.

Bezemer, P.-J., Nicholson, G., & Pugliese, A. (2018). The influence of board chairs on director engagement: A case-based exploration of boardroom decision-making. *Corporate Governance: An International Review*, **26**(3), 219–34.

Black, B. S., Cheffins, B. R., & Klausner, M. (2006). Outside director liability: A policy analysis. *Journal of Institutional and Theoretical Economics*, **162** (1), 5–20. https://doi.org/info:doi/10.1628/093245606776166543.

Blair, M. M. (1995). *Ownership and Control: Rethinking Corporate Governance for the 21st Century*. Washington, DC: Brookings Institution.

Blair, M. M. (1998). For whom should corporations be run?: An economic rationale for stakeholder management. *Long Range Planning*, **31**(2), 195–200. https://doi.org/10.1016/S0024-6301(98)00003-X.

Blair, M. M., & Stout, L. A. (1999). A team production theory of corporate law. *Virginia Law Review*, **85**(2), 247–328. https://doi.org/10.2307/1073662.

Blair, M. M., & Stout, L. A. (2001). Director accountability and the mediating role of the corporate board. *Washington University Law Quarterly*, **79**(2), 403–48.

Bolton, P., Brunnermeier, M. K., & Veldkamp, L. (2010). Economists' perspectives on leadership. In N. Nohria and R. Khurana, eds, *Handbook of Leadership Theory and Practice*. Boston, MA: Harvard Business Press, pp. 239–64.

Bolton, P., Brunnermeier, M. K., & Veldkamp, L. (2012). Leadership, coordination, and corporate culture. *Review of Economic Studies*, **80**(2), 512–37.

Bryman, A., Collinson, D., Grint, K., Jackson, B., & Uhl-Bien, M. (eds). (2011). *The SAGE Handbook of Leadership*. London: SAGE Publications.

Burkart, M., Gromb, D., & Panunzi, F. (1997). Large shareholders, monitoring, and the value of the firm. *The Quarterly Journal of Economics*, **112**(3), 693–728. https://doi.org/10.1162/003355397555325.

Carter, C., & Lorsch, J. W. (2004). *Back to the Drawing Board: Designing Corporate Boards for a Complex World*. Boston: Harvard Business Press.

Cartwright, D. (1965). Influence, leadership, control. In J. March, ed., *Handbook of Organizations*. Chicago: Rand McNally, pp.1–47.

Casal, C., & Caspar, C. (2014). Building a forward-looking board. *McKinsey Quarterly*, **2**, 119–26.

Chait, R. P., Ryan, W. P., & Taylor, B. E. (2005). *Governance as Leadership: Reframing the Work of Nonprofit Boards*. Hoboken, NJ: John Wiley & Sons.

Cikaliuk, M., Eraković, L., Jackson, B., Noonan, C., & Watson, S. (2018a). Board leadership and governance for clear-sighted CEO succession at Air New Zealand. *Journal of Management & Organization*, 1–24. https://doi.org/10.1017/jmo.2018.23.

Cikaliuk, M., Eraković, L., Jackson, B., Noonan, C., & Watson, S. (2018b). Leadership in governance: Women board chairs. In L. Devnew, M. J. Le Ber, M. Torchia and R. J. Burke, eds, *More Women on Boards: An International Perspective*. Charlotte, NC: Information Age Publishing, pp. 269–83.

Clark V. Workman, 1920 IR 1 (1920).

Clarke, T. (2013). Deconstructing the mythology of shareholder value: A comment on Lynn Stout's 'The Shareholder Value Myth'. *Accounting, Economics, and Law; Berlin*, **3**(1), 15–42. http://dx.doi.org.ezproxy.auckland.ac.nz/10.1515/ael-2013-0006.

Clarke, T. (2014). Dangerous frontiers in corporate governance. *Journal of Management & Organization*, **20**(03), 268–86. https://doi.org/10.1017/jmo.2014.37.

Clarke, T. (2017). *International Corporate Governance: A Comparative Approach*, 2nd edn. London: Routledge.

Clegg, S., & Bailey, J. R. (2007). *International Encyclopedia of Organization Studies*. Thousand Oaks, CA: SAGE Publications.

Conger, J. A., & Lawler, E. E. (2009a). Sharing leadership on corporate boards: A critical requirement for teamwork at the top. *Organizational Dynamics*, **38**(3), 183–91. https://doi.org/10.1016/j.orgdyn.2009.04.007.

Conger, J. A., & Lawler, E. E. (2009b). Why your board needs a non-executive chair. In J. A. Conger, ed., *Boardroom Realities: Building Leaders across Your Board*. San Francisco: Jossey-Bass Publishers, pp. 51–67.

Creswell, J. W., & Poth, C. N. (2017). *Qualitative Inquiry and Research Design: Choosing Among Five Approaches*, 4th edn. Los Angeles: SAGE Publications.

Dailey, P. R., & Koblentz, J. M. (2012). Refreshing your board of directors – What if you shook up board membership and processes before a crisis strikes? *Corporate Board*, **33**(197), 16–20.

Davies, A. (2006). *Best Practice in Corporate Governance: Building Reputation and Sustainable Success*. Aldershot: Gower.

Davies, P. L., & Worthington, S. (2008). *Gower and Davies' Principles of Company Law*, 8th edn. London: Sweet & Maxwell.

Davis, G. F. (2016). *The Vanishing American Corporation: Navigating the Hazards of a New Economy*. Oakland, CA: Berrett-Koehler Publishers.

Deakin, S. (2019). The evolution of corporate form: From shareholders property to the corporation as commons. In T. Clarke, J. O'Brien and C. O'Kelley, eds. *The Oxford Handbook of the Corporation*. Oxford: Oxford University Press, pp. 687–710.

Deakin, S., Gindis, D., Hodgson, G. M., Huang, K., & Pistor, K. (2017). Legal institutionalism: Capitalism and the constitutive role of law. *Journal of Comparative Economics*, **45**(1), 188–200. https://doi.org/10.1016/j.jce.2016.04.005.

Deloitte Development LLC. (2016). Board Effectiveness: A Focus on Behavior. Retrieved 4 December 2018, from www2.deloitte.com/us/en/pages/center-for-board-effectiveness/articles/board-effectiveness-a-focus-on-behavior.html.

Dewan, T., & Myatt, D. P. (2008). The qualities of leadership: Direction, communication, and obfuscation. *American Political Science Review*, **102**(3), 351–68.

Dinh, J. E., Lord, R. G., Gardner, W. L., et al. (2014). Leadership theory and research in the new millennium: Current theoretical trends and changing perspectives. *The Leadership Quarterly*, **25**(1), 36–62.

Dodd Jr, E. M. (1932). For whom are corporate managers trustees? *Harvard Law Review*, **45**(7), 1145–63.

Donaldson, T., & Preston, L. E. (1995). The stakeholder theory of the corporation: Concepts, evidence, and implications. *The Academy of Management Review*, **20**(1), 65–91. https://doi.org/10.2307/258887.

Easterbrook, F. H., & Fischel, D. R. (1996). *The Economic Structure of Corporate Law*. Cambridge, MA: Harvard University Press.

Ees, H. van, Gabrielsson, J., & Huse, M. (2009). Toward a behavioral theory of boards and corporate governance. *Corporate Governance: An International Review*, **17**(3), 307–19.

Eisenberg, M. A. (1989). The structure of corporation law. *Columbia Law Review*, **89**(7), 1461–525.

Eisenhardt, K. M. (1989). Agency theory: An assessment and review. *Academy of Management Review*, **14**(1), 57–74.

Engelen, A., Gupta, V., Strenger, L., & Brettel, M. (2015). Entrepreneurial orientation, firm performance, and the moderating role of transformational leadership behaviors. *Journal of Management*, **41**(4), 1069–97. https://doi.org/10.1177/0149206312455244.

Erakovic, L., & Jackson, B. (2012). Promoting leadership in governance and governance in leadership: Towards a supportive research agenda. In A. Davila, M. M. Elvira, J. Ramirez and L. Zapata-Cantu, eds, *Understanding Organizations in Complex, Emergent and Uncertain Environments*. Basingstoke: Palgrave Macmillan, pp. 68–83. https://doi.org/10.1057/9781137026088_4.

Esser, I., & du Plessis, J. J. (2007). The stakeholder debate and directors' fiduciary duties. *South African Mercantile Law Journal*, **19**(3), 346–63.

Fassin, Y. (2009). The stakeholder model refined. *Journal of Business Ethics*, **84** (1), 113–35.

Ferreira, D., & Rezende, M. (2007). Corporate strategy and information disclosure. *The RAND Journal of Economics*, **38**(1), 164–84.

Fhr European Ventures Llp v. Cedar Capital Partners LLC, 2014 UKSC (2014).

Filatotchev, I., & Nakajima, C. (2014). Corporate governance, responsible managerial behavior, and corporate social responsibility: Organizational efficiency versus organizational legitimacy? *Academy of Management Perspectives*, **28**(3), 289–306.

Filatotchev, I., Toms, S., & Wright, M. (2006). The firm's strategic dynamics and corporate governance life-cycle. *International Journal of Managerial Finance*, **2**(4), 256–79.

Financial Reporting Council. (2018). The UK Corporate Governance Code. Financial Reporting Council. Retrieved 12 March 2020 from www.frc.org.uk /getattachment/59a5171d-4163-4fb2-9e9d-daefcd7153b5/UK-Corporate-Governance-Code-2014.pdf.

Finkelstein, S., Hambrick, D. C., & Cannella, A. A. (2009). *Strategic Leadership: Theory and Research on Executives, Top Management Teams, and Boards*. New York: Oxford University Press.

Finkelstein, S., & Mooney, A. C. (2003). Not the usual suspects: How to use board process to make boards better. *Academy of Management Perspectives*, **17**(2), 101–13. https://doi.org/10.5465/ame.2003.10025204.

Forbes, D. P., & Milliken, F. J. (1999). Cognition and corporate governance: Understanding boards of directors as strategic decision-making groups. *Academy of Management Review*, **24**(3), 489–505.

Freeman, R. E. (1984). *Strategic Management: A Stakeholder Approach*. Boston: Pittman Books.

Freeman, R. E., Harrison, J. S., & Zyglidopoulos, S. (2018). *Stakeholder Theory: Concepts and Strategies*. Cambridge: Cambridge University Press.

French, J. R., & Raven, B. (1959). The bases of social power. In D. Cartwright, ed., *Studies in Social Power*. Ann Arbor, MI: Institute for Social Research, University of Michigan, pp.150–67.

Fulham Football Club Ltd v. Cabra Estates plc, 1994 BCLC 1 (1994).

Gabrielsson, J., Huse, M., & Minichilli, A. (2007). Understanding the leadership role of the board chairperson through a team production approach. *International Journal of Leadership Studies*, **3**(1), 21–39.

Gardner, W. L., Lowe, K. B., Moss, T. W., Mahoney, K. T., & Cogliser, C. C. (2010). Scholarly leadership of the study of leadership: A review of *The Leadership Quarterly*'s second decade, 2000–2009. *The Leadership Quarterly*, **21**(6), 922–58.

Gautier, A. (2002). Men behaving badly. *New Zealand Management*, **49**(4), 26–31.

Geletkanycz, M. A., & Hambrick, D. C. (1997). The external ties of top executives: Implications for strategic choice and performance. *Administrative Science Quarterly*, **42**(4), 654–81.

Gervais, S., & Goldstein, I. (2007). The positive effects of biased self-perceptions in firms. *Review of Finance*, **11**(3), 453–96.

Gibby, T. (2016, June 14). Effective Board Leadership Is Like … Retrieved 4 December 2018, from www.boardeffect.com/blog/effective-board-leadership-is-like/.

Gibson, K. (2000). The moral basis of stakeholder theory. *Journal of Business Ethics*, **26**(3), 245–57.

Goel, A. M., & Thakor, A. V. (2008). Overconfidence, CEO selection, and corporate governance. *The Journal of Finance*, **63**(6), 2737–84.

Gray, J. (2007). Myths and reality. *Canadian Business*, **80**(16/17), 60–3.

Gunasekara, G. (2013). Privacy as a stakeholder interest in New Zealand: Transparency in corporate governance practices. *New Zealand Business Law Quarterly*, **19**(4), 271–94.

Hambrick, D. C., & Mason, P. A. (1984). Upper echelons: The organization as a reflection of its top managers. *Academy of Management Review*, **9**(2), 193–206.

Harrison, J. S., & Wicks, A. C. (2013). Stakeholder theory, value, and firm performance. *Business Ethics Quarterly*, **23**(1), 97–124.

Harrison, Y. D., & Murray, V. (2012). Perspectives on the leadership of chairs of nonprofit organization boards of directors: A grounded theory mixed-method study. *Nonprofit Management and Leadership*, **22**(4), 411–37. https://doi.org/10.1002/nml.21038.

Heenan, D. A., & Bennis, W. (1999). *Co-Leaders: The Power of Great Partnerships*. New York: Wiley.

Hendry, K. P., Kiel, G. C., & Nicholson, G. (2010). How boards strategise: A strategy as practice view. *Long Range Planning*, **43**(1), 33–56. https://doi.org/10.1016/j.lrp.2009.09.005.

Hermalin, B. E. (1998). Toward an economic theory of leadership: Leading by example. *The American Economic Review*, **88**(5), 1188–206.

Hermalin, B. E. (2007). Leading for the long term. *Journal of Economic Behavior & Organization*, **62**(1), 1–19.

Holloway, D. A., & van Rhyn, D. (2005). Effective corporate governance reform and organisational pluralism: Reframing culture, leadership and followership. In C. Lehman, ed., *Corporate Governance: Does Any Size Fit?* Vol. 11. Amsterdam: Emerald Group Publishing Limited, pp. 303–28.

Howard Smith Ltd v. Ampol Petroleum Ltd, 1974 AC (1974).

Huck, S., & Rey-Biel, P. (2006). Endogenous leadership in teams. *Journal of Institutional and Theoretical Economics (JITE)/Zeitschrift Für Die Gesamte Staatswissenschaft*, **162**(2), 253–61. https://doi.org/DOI:info:doi/10.1628/093245606777583495.

Hung, H. (2011). Directors' roles in corporate social responsibility: A stakeholder perspective. *Journal of Business Ethics*, **103**(3), 385–402. https://doi.org/10.1007/s10551-011-0870-5.

Huse, M. (1994). Board-management relations in small firms: The paradox of simultaneous independence and interdependence. *Small Business Economics*, **6**(1), 55–72.

Huse, M. (2005). Accountability and creating accountability: A framework for exploring behavioural perspectives of corporate governance. *British Journal of Management*, **16**(s1), S65–S79. https://doi.org/10.1111/j.1467-8551.2005.00448.x.

Huse, M. (2007). *Boards, Governance and Value Creation: The Human Side of Corporate Governance*. New York: Cambridge University Press.

Huse, M. (ed.). (2009). *The Value Creating Board: Corporate Governance and Organizational Behaviour*. New York: Routledge.

Huse, M. (2018). Value-creating boards: Challenges for future research and practice. In T. Clarke, ed., *Cambridge Elements in Corporate Governance*. Cambridge: Cambridge University Press. https://doi.org/10.1017/9781108564786.

Huse, M., & Gabrielsson, J. (2012). Board leadership and value creation: An extended team production approach. In T. Clarke and D. M. Branson, eds., *The SAGE Handbook of Corporate Governance*. London: SAGE Publications, pp. 233–52. https://doi.org/10.4135/9781446200995.n12.

Huse, M., Gabrielsson, J., & Minichilli, A. (2009). How board contribute to value creation. In M. Huse, ed., *The Value Creating Board: Corporate Governance and Organizational Behaviour*. New York: Routledge, pp. 523–32.

Huse, M., & Rindova, V. P. (2001). Stakeholders' expectations of board roles: The case of subsidiary boards. *Journal of Management and Governance*, **5**(2), 153–78.

Huse, M., & Zattoni, A. (2008). Trust, firm life cycle, and actual board behavior: Evidence from 'one of the lads' in the board of three small firms. *International Studies of Management & Organization*, **38**(3), 71–97.

Huxham, C., & Vangen, S. (2000). Leadership in the shaping and implementation of collaboration agendas: How things happen in a (not quite) joined-up world. *Academy of Management Journal*, **43**(6), 1159–75.

In Re Smith and Fawcett Ltd, 1942 Ch (1942).

In Re Westmid Packing Services Ltd, 1998 All ER 2 (1998).

Ingley, C., Rennie, M., Mueller, J., et al. (2011). Reformed and engaged boards–not activist shareholders. *World Review of Entrepreneurship, Management and Sustainable Development*, **7**(3), 302–29. https://doi.org/10.1504/WREMSD.2011.040811.

Institute of Chartered Secretaries and Administrators & The Investment Association. (2017). *The Stakeholder Voice in Board Decision Making: Strengthening the Business, Promoting Long-Term Success*. London:Institute of Chartered Secretaries and Administrators & The Investment Association. Retrieved 12 March 2020, from www.icsa.org.uk/assets/files/free-guidance-notes/the-stakeholder-voice-in-Board-Decision-Making-09-2017.pdf.

Institute of Corporate Directors, Canada. (2015). Beyond Term Limits: Using Performance Management to Guide Board Renewal. Retrieved 12 December 2018, from www.icd.ca/getmedia/e57f3478-2b5c-4f14-aad4-5aa8d6a7298d/15-1889-Beyond_Term_Limits_EN_Final.pdf.aspx.

International Integrated Reporting Council. (2018). Get to Grips with the Six Capitals. Retrieved 5 April 2018, from https://integratedreporting.org/what-the-tool-for-better-reporting/get-to-grips-with-the-six-capitals/.

Jackson, B., & Parry, K. (2018). *A Very Short Fairly Interesting and Reasonably Cheap Book about Studying Leadership*, 3rd ed. London: SAGE Publications.

Jensen, M. (2001). Value maximisation, stakeholder theory, and the corporate objective function. *European Financial Management*, **7**(3), 297–317. https://doi.org/10.1111/1468-036X.00158.

Jensen, M. C., & Meckling, W. H. (1976). Theory of the firm: Managerial behavior, agency costs and ownership structure. *Journal of Financial Economics*, **3**(4), 305–60.

Judge, T. A., & Piccolo, R. F. (2004). Transformational and transactional leadership: A meta-analytic test of their relative validity. *Journal of Applied Psychology*, **89**(5), 755–68.

Jung, D. I., & Avolio, B. J. (2000). Opening the black box: An experimental investigation of the mediating effects of trust and value congruence on transformational and transactional leadership. *Journal of Organizational*

Behavior, **21**(8), 949–64. https://doi.org/10.1002/1099-1379(200012) 21:8<949::aid-job64>3.0.CO;2-F.

Jung, D. I., & Sosik, J. J. (2002). Transformational leadership in work groups: The role of empowerment, cohesiveness, and collective-efficacy on perceived group performance. *Small Group Research*, **33**(3), 313–36. https://doi .org/10.1177/10496402033003002.

Kakabadse, A., Kakabadse, N. K., & Barratt, R. (2006). Chairman and chief executive officer (CEO): That sacred and secret relationship. *Journal of Management Development*, **25**(2), 134–50.

Kaler, J. (2003). Differentiating stakeholder theories. *Journal of Business Ethics*, **46**(1), 71–83. https://doi.org/10.1023/A:1024794710899.

Kaufman, A., & Englander, E. (2005). A team production model of corporate governance. *The Academy of Management Executive*, **19**(3), 9–22.

Khanna, P., Jones, C. D., & Boivie, S. (2014). Director human capital, information processing demands, and board effectiveness. *Journal of Management*, **40**(2), 557–85.

Klarner, P., Yoshikawa, T., & Hitt, M. A. (2018). A capability-based view of boards: A new conceptual framework for board governance. *Academy of Management Perspectives*, forthcoming. https://doi.org/10.5465/amp.2017.0030.

Knippenberg, D. van, & Sitkin, S. B. (2013). A critical assessment of charismatic – transformational leadership research: Back to the drawing board? *The Academy of Management Annals*, **7**(1), 1–60.

Knoll, M. S. (2018). The Modigliani–Miller theorem at 60: The long-overlooked legal applications of finance's foundational theorem. *Yale Journal on Regulation Bulletin*, **36**, 1–21.

Kobayashi, H., & Suehiro, H. (2005). Emergence of leadership in teams. *The Japanese Economic Review*, **56**(3), 295–316.

Kocourek, P., Burger, C., & Birchard, B. (2003). Hard facts: Soft behaviours. *New Zealand Management*, **50**(7), 68–9.

Kor, Y. Y., & Sundaramurthy, C. (2009). Experience-based human capital and social capital of outside directors. *Journal of Management*, **35**(4), 981–1006.

Kortmann, S., & Piller, F. (2016). Open business models and closed-loop value chains: Redefining the firm-consumer relationship. *California Management Review*, **58**(3), 88–108.

Kraakman, R., Armour, J., Davies, P., et al. (2017). *The Anatomy of Corporate Law: A Comparative and Functional Approach*, 3rd ed. New York: Oxford University Press.

Kraatz, M. S., & Block, E. S. (2008). Organizational implications of institutional pluralism. In R. Greenwood, C. Oliver, K. Sahlin and R. Suddaby, eds,

The SAGE Handbook of Organizational Institutionalism. London: SAGE Publications, pp. 243–75.

Langley, A. (1999). Strategies for theorizing from process data. *Academy of Management Review*, **24**(4), 691–710.

Langley, A., Smallman, C., Tsoukas, H., & van de Ven, A. H. (2013). Process studies of change in organization and management: Unveiling temporality, activity, and flow. *Academy of Management Journal*, **56**(1), 1–13.

Leblanc, R. (2005). Assessing board leadership. *Corporate Governance: An International Review*, **13**(5), 654–66.

Leblanc, R., & Gillies, J. (2005). *Inside the Boardroom: How Boards Really Work and the Coming Revolution in Corporate Governance*. Mississauga, Ontario Canada: John Wiley & Sons.

Letza, S., Sun, X., & Kirkbride, J. (2004). Shareholding versus stakeholding: A critical review of corporate governance. *Corporate Governance*, **12**(3), 242–62. https://doi.org/10.1111/j.1467-8683.2004.00367.x.

Levrau, A., & van den Berghe, L. (2013). Perspectives on the decision-making style of the board chair. *International Journal of Disclosure and Governance*, **10**(2), 105–21.

Lim, E. (2015). Contracting out of fiduciary duties. *Common Law World Review*, **44**(4), 276–97. https://doi.org/10.1177/1473779515616035.

Lorsch, J. W. (2009). Leadership: The key to effective boards. In J. A. Conger, ed., *Boardroom Realities: Building Leaders Across Your Board*. San Francisco: Jossey-Bass Publishers, pp. 25–50.

Lorsch, J. W. (2017). Understanding boards of directors: A systems perspective. *Annals of Corporate Governance*, **2**(1), 1–49. https://doi.org/10.1561/109.00000006.

Lorsch, J. W., & Clark, R. C. (2008). Leading from the boardroom. *Harvard Business Review*, **86**(4), 104–11.

Lorsch, J. W., & MacIver, E. (1989). *Pawns or Potentates: The Reality of America's Corporate Boards*. Boston: Harvard Business School Press.

Lynall, M. D., Golden, B. R., & Hillman, A. J. (2003). Board composition from adolescence to maturity: A multitheoretic view. *Academy of Management Review*, **28**(3), 416–31.

Machold, S., & Farquhar, S. (2013). Board task evolution: A longitudinal field study in the UK: Board task evolution. *Corporate Governance: An International Review*, **21**(2), 147–64. https://doi.org/10.1111/corg.12017.

Machold, S., Huse, M., Minichilli, A., & Nordqvist, M. (2011). Board leadership and strategy involvement in small firms: A team production approach. *Corporate Governance: An International Review*, **19**(4), 368–83. https://doi.org/10.1111/j.1467-8683.2011.00852.x.

Madoff Securities International Ltd v. Raven, 2013 EWHC (2013).

Maharaj, R. (2008). Critiquing and contrasting 'moral' stakeholder theory and 'strategic' stakeholder: Implications for the board of directors. *Corporate Governance: The International Journal of Business in Society*, **8**(2), 115–27. https://doi.org/10.1108/14720700810863751.

March, J. G. (1991). Exploration and exploitation in organizational learning. *Organization Science*, **2**(1), 71–87.

McDonald, M. L., Khanna, P., & Westphal, J. D. (2008). Getting them to think outside the circle: Corporate governance, CEOs' external advice networks, and firm performance. *Academy of Management Journal*, **51**(3), 453–75. https://doi.org/10.5465/amj.2008.32625969.

McGregor, L. (2000). *The Human Face of Corporate Governance*. New York: Palgrave.

McNulty, T., & Pettigrew, A. (1999). Strategists on the board. *Organization Studies*, **20**(1), 47–74. https://doi.org/10.1177/0170840699201003.

McNulty, T., Pettigrew, A., Jobome, G., & Morris, C. (2011). The role, power and influence of company chairs. *Journal of Management & Governance*, **15**(1), 91–121.

Mehra, A., Smith, B. R., Dixon, A. L., & Robertson, B. (2006). Distributed leadership in teams: The network of leadership perceptions and team performance. *The Leadership Quarterly*, **17**(3), 232–45.

Meridian Global Funds Management Asia Ltd v. Securities Commission, 1995 AC 2 (1995).

Miles, M. B., & Huberman, M. A. (1994). *Qualitative Data Analysis: An Expanded Sourcebook*, 2nd edn. London: SAGE Publications.

Minichilli, A., Zattoni, A., Nielsen, S., & Huse, M. (2012). Board task performance: An exploration of micro- and macro-level determinants of board effectiveness. *Journal of Organizational Behavior*, **33**(2), 193–215. https://doi.org/10.1002/job.743.

Moore, M. T. (2014). Private ordering and public policy: The paradoxical foundations of corporate contractarianism. *Oxford Journal of Legal Studies*, **34**(4), 693–728. https://doi.org/10.1093/ojls/gqu006.

Morgan, G. (1997). *Images of Organizations*, 2nd edn. London: SAGE Publications.

Nicholson, G., Pugliese, A., & Bezemer, P.-J. (2017). Habitual accountability routines in the boardroom: How boards balance control and collaboration. *Accounting, Auditing & Accountability Journal*, **30**(2), 222–46.

Nicholson, G. J., Alexander, M., & Kiel, G. C. (2004). Defining the social capital of the board of directors: An exploratory study. *Journal of*

Management & Organization, **10**(1), 54–72. https://doi.org/10.1017 /S1833367200004612.

Nooteboom, B. (1996). Trust, opportunism and governance: A process and control model. *Organization Studies*, **17**(6), 985–1011.

Official Receiver v. Watson, 2008 EWHC (2008).

O'Toole, J., Galbraith, J., & Lawler III, E. E. (2002). When two (or more) heads are better than one: The promise and pitfalls of shared leadership. *California Management Review*, **44**(4), 65–83.

Pearce, C. L., & Conger, J. A. (2003). All those years ago: The historical underpinnings of shared leadership. In C. L. Pearce and J. A. Conger, eds, *Shared Leadership: Reframing the Hows and Whys of Leadership*. Thousand Oaks, CA: SAGE Publications, pp. 1–18.

Pearce, C. L., Conger, J. A., & Locke, E. A. (2008). Shared leadership theory. *The Leadership Quarterly*, **19**(5), 622–8.

Pearce, C. L., & Sims, H. P. (2000). Shared leadership: Toward a multi-level theory of leadership. *Advances in Interdisciplinary Studies of Work Teams*. Vol. 7. Bingley: Emerald Group Publishing Limited, pp. 115–39.

Perrault, E., & McHugh, P. (2015). Toward a life cycle theory of board evolution: Considering firm legitimacy. *Journal of Management & Organization*, **21**(5), 627–49. https://doi.org/10.1017/jmo.2014.92.

Pettigrew, A. M. (1992). On studying managerial elites. *Strategic Management Journal*, **13**(Special Issue), 163–82.

Pettigrew, A. M., & McNulty, T. (1995). Power and influence in and around the boardroom. *Human Relations*, **48**(8), 845–73. https://doi.org/10.1177 /001872679504800802.

Plessis, J. J. du (2016). Shareholder primacy and other stakeholder interests. *Company and Securities Law Journal*, **34**, 238–42.

Plessis, J. J. du (2017). Corporate social responsibility and contemporary community expectations. *Company and Securities Law Journal*, **35**, 30–47.

Prahalad, C. K., & Ramaswamy, V. (2000). Co-opting customer competence. *Harvard Business Review*, **78**(1), 79–90.

Pugliese, A., Bezemer, P-J., Zattoni, A., et al. (2009). Boards of directors' contribution to strategy: A literature review and research agenda. *Corporate Governance: An International Review*, **17**(3), 292–306. https://doi .org/10.1111/j.1467-8683.2009.00740.x.

Pye, A. (2002). Corporate directing: Governing, strategising and leading in action. *Corporate Governance: An International Review*, **10**(3), 153–62. https://doi.org/10.1111/1467-8683.00280.

Ravasi, D., & Zattoni, A. (2006). Exploring the political side of board involvement in strategy: A study of mixed-ownership institutions. *Journal of Management Studies*, **43**(8), 1671–702.

Robé, J-P. (2011). The legal structure of the firm. *Accounting, Economics, and Law*, **1**(1), 1–86.

Roberts, J., McNulty, T., & Stiles, P. (2005). Beyond agency conceptions of the work of the non-executive director: Creating accountability in the boardroom. *British Journal of Management*, **16**(S1), S5–S26. https://doi.org/10.1111/j.1467-8551.2005.00444.x.

Roberts, J., & Stiles, P. (1999). The relationship between chairmen and chief executives: Competitive or complementary roles? *Long Range Planning*, **32**(1), 36–48.

Rost, J. C. (1993). *Leadership for the Twenty-First Century*. Westport, CT: Greenwood Publishing Group.

Rotemberg, J. J., & Saloner, G. (1993). Leadership style and incentives. *Management Science*, **39**(11), 1299–318.

Sally, D. (2002). Co-leadership: Lessons from republican Rome. *California Management Review*, **44**(4), 84–99.

Salomon's Case, 1897 AC (1897).

Schyns, B., & Schilling, J. (2013). How bad are the effects of bad leaders? A meta-analysis of destructive leadership and its outcomes. *The Leadership Quarterly*, **24**(1), 138–58.

Siciliano, J. I. (2005). Board involvement in strategy and organisational performance. *Journal of General Management*, **30**(4), 1–10. https://doi.org/10.1177/030630700503000401.

Sjåfjell, B. (2016). Achieving corporate sustainability: What is the role of the shareholder? In H. S. Birkmose, ed., *Shareholders' Duties*. Vol. 12 of European Company Law Series. Alphen aan den Rijn: Kluwer Law International, pp.377–404.

SpencerStuart. (2018). 2018 U.S. Spencer Stuart Board Index. Retrieved 12 December 2018, from https://www.spencerstuart.com/-/media/2018/december/ukbi2018_8b.pdf.

Steen, E. van den (2005). Organizational beliefs and managerial vision. *Journal of Law, Economics, and Organization*, **21**(1), 256–83.

Stiles, P., & Taylor, B. (2001). *Boards at Work: How Directors View Their Roles and Responsibilities*. New York: Oxford University Press.

Stout, L. A. (2012). *The Shareholder Value Myth: How Putting Shareholders First Harms Investors, Corporations, and the Public*. San Francisco: Berrett-Koehler Publishers.

Strine Jr, L. E. (2014). Can we do better by ordinary investors: A pragmatic reaction to the dueling ideological mythologists of corporate law. *Columbia Law Review*, **114**, 449–502.

Summers, R. S. (1968). 'Good faith' in general contract law and the sales provisions of the uniform commercial code. *Virginia Law Review*, **54**(2), 195–267.

Sundaramurthy, C., & Lewis, M. (2003). Control and collaboration: Paradoxes of governance. *Academy of Management Review*, **28**(3), 397–415.

Thorby v. Goldberg, 112 CLR (1964).

Thorpe, R., Gold, J., & Lawler, J. (2011). Locating distributed leadership. *International Journal of Management Reviews*, **13**(3), 239–50.

Tourish, D. (2013). *The Dark Side of Transformational Leadership: A Critical Perspective*. London: Routledge.

Tricker, B. (1994). *International Corporate Governance: Text, Readings, and Cases*. New York: Prentice Hall.

Tricker, B. (2000). Corporate governance – the subject whose time has come. *Corporate Governance: An International Review*, **8**(4), 289–96.

Useem, M., Carey, D., & Charan, R. (2016). Board That Lead. In R. Leblanc, ed., *The Handbook of Board Governance: A Comprehensive Guide for Public, Private and Not for Profit Board Members*. Hoboken, NJ: John Wiley & Sons, pp. 26–45.

Vaara, E., Sonenshein, S., & Boje, D. (2016). Narratives as sources of stability and change in organizations: Approaches and directions for future research. *The Academy of Management Annals*, **10**(1), 495–560.

Vandewaerde, M., Voordeckers, W., Lambrechts, F., & Bammens, Y. (2011). Board team leadership revisited: A conceptual model of shared leadership in the boardroom. *Journal of Business Ethics*, **104**(3), 403–20. https://doi.org/10.1007/s10551-011-0918-6.

Vasudev, P. M. (2012). Corporate stakeholders in New Zealand – The present, and possibilities for the future. *New Zealand Business Law Quarterly*, **18**(2), 167–80.

Vasudev, P. M. (2013). Corporate stakeholders in Canada – An overview and a proposal. *Ottawa Law Review*, **45**(1), 137–80.

Wang, G., Oh, I.-S., Courtright, S. H., & Colbert, A. E. (2011). Transformational leadership and performance across criteria and levels: A meta-analytic review of 25 years of research. *Group & Organization Management*, **36**(2), 223–70.

Watson, S. (2015). How the company became an entity: A new understanding of corporate law. *Journal of Business Law*, **120**, 1–24.

Watson, S. (2018). The corporate legal person. *Journal of Corporate Law Studies*, forthcoming, https://doi.org/10.1080/14735970.2018.1435951.

Weinstein, O. (2013). The shareholder model of the corporation, between mythology and reality. *Accounting, Economics and Law*, **3**(1), 43–60. https://doi.org/10.1515/ael-2013-0032.

Westphal, J. D., & Zajac, E. J. (2013). A behavioral theory of corporate governance: Explicating the mechanisms of socially situated and socially constituted agency. *The Academy of Management Annals*, **7**(1), 607–61.

Wilson, S., Cummings, S., Jackson, B., & Proctor-Thomson, S. (2018). Revitalising or revolutionising? Leadership scholarship. In *Revitalising Leadership: Putting Theory and Practice into Context*. London: Routledge, pp.181–96.

Yar Hamidi, D., & Gabrielsson, J. (2014a). Developments and trends in research on board leadership: A systematic literature review. *International Journal of Business Governance and Ethics*, **9**(3), 243–68. https://doi.org/10.1504/IJBGE.2014.064739.

Yar Hamidi, D., & Gabrielsson, J. (2014b). *Board Chairmanship and Innovation in Growth Oriented Firms: Opening Up the Black box Of Leadership in the Boardroom*. Presented at the EURAM conference, Valencia, Spain.

Yukl, G. A. (2013). *Leadership in Organizations*, 8th edn. Boston: Pearson Education.

Zahra, S. A., & Filatotchev, I. (2004). Governance of the entrepreneurial threshold firm: A knowledge-based perspective. *Journal of Management Studies*, **41**(5), 885–97.

Zahra, S. A., & Newey, L. R. (2009). Maximizing the impact of organization science: Theory-building at the intersection of disciplines and/or fields. *Journal of Management Studies*, **46**(6), 1059–75. https://doi.org/10.1111/j.1467-6486.2009.00848.x.

Zahra, S. A., & Pearce, J. A. (1989). Boards of directors and corporate financial performance: A review and integrative model. *Journal of Management*, **15**(2), 291–334.

Zupan, M. A. (2010). An economic perspective on leadership. In N. Nohria and R. Khurana, eds. *Handbook of Leadership Theory and Practice*. Boston: Harvard Business Press, pp. 265–90.

Acknowledgements

We are grateful to the University of Auckland Business School for providing support for this research project. We would also like to thank Thomas Clarke for his patient and persistent support throughout the compilation of this contribution.

We acknowledge with appreciation the contributions of research participants who generously shared their insights into the practice of board leadership.

Cambridge Elements ≡

Corporate Governance

Thomas Clarke

UTS Business School, University of Technology Sydney

Thomas Clarke is Professor of Corporate Governance at the UTS Business School of the University of Technology Sydney. His work focuses on the institutional diversity of corporate governance and his most recent book is *International Corporate Governance* (Second Edition 2017). He is interested in questions about the purposes of the corporation, and the convergence of the concerns of corporate governance and corporate sustainability.

About the series

The series Elements in Corporate Governance focuses on the significant emerging field of corporate governance. Authoritative, lively and compelling analyses include expert surveys of the foundations of the discipline, original insights into controversial debates, frontier developments, and masterclasses on key issues. Its areas of interest include empirical studies of corporate governance in practice, regional institutional diversity, emerging fields, key problems and core theoretical perspectives.

Cambridge Elements ☰

Corporate Governance

Elements in the series

Printed in the United States
By Bookmasters